HOOF-BEATS
THROUGH MY HEART

A life shared with horses

*David Edelsten on the roguish Ollie, on loan to the author
for the hunting season 2008-9*

HOOF-BEATS
THROUGH MY HEART

A life shared with horses

DAVID EDELSTEN

Merlin Unwin Books

First published in Great Britain by Merlin Unwin Books, 2012

Text © David Edelsten, 2012

Merlin Unwin Books Ltd
Palmers House
7 Corve Street
Ludlow, Shropshire SY8 1DB
U.K.

www.merlinunwin.co.uk
email: books@merlinunwin.co.uk

The author asserts his moral right to be identified as the author of this work.
A CIP catalogue record for this book is available from the British Library.
ISBN 978-1-906122-44-7
Designed and set in Bembo by Merlin Unwin
Printed and bound by Jellyfish Print Solutions

Contents

Foreword by Lucy Higginson

Horses have been laced through David's life – truly hoof-beats through his heart – as a constant source of pleasure, companionship, respite and insight. From his first pony, Cherrypie, to his final homebred hunters, David describes them with the fondness one reserves for the closest friends, chuckling over their idiosyncracies, and sharing the lessons he learnt from them. There's Fortuna, his regimental ride in Germany, who taught him 'to guide, trust and talk to her, rather than fight her'. And Daisy, who was a disaster in the Army saddle club, but who bloomed in David's private ownership (and who later had her owner, the Brigadier, 'all but blubbing like a baby' on her final journey to the Kennels).

Impeccably penned, their portraits will strike chords with every fellow rider. Consider Bella, for example, who 'takes fright at the most ridiculous things, such as if a gnat should happen to clear its throat in the hedge'.

As a rider, David claims just 'to get by, with horses more or less doing what I want them to do.' It's the only time I have ever doubted the accuracy of his writing, flicking to a nearby photograph that shows him sailing over a hunting fence in his 76th year.

Some great horsemen believe that horses tend to mirror the personalities of their owners; David has found – and bred – a suspiciously large number of generous, bold and enthusiastic hunters for the moderate horseman he claims to be. Besides, would a dunce ever have survived 'well over 120 outings with 67 different hunts, on 64 different horses' which David says he has chalked up?

'If you learn nothing else as a soldier you learn to prize comradeship, a good working relationship with those around you based on mutual, well-tried and well-founded reliance, and that rare, precious, thing, utter dependability,' writes David. He is thinking of his horses again, but this, I feel, might be his mantra for life, for all that I've only known him through his third and final career, as a hunting scribe and general editor's godsend.

'Will you come for a last ride with me?' asks David in the final chapter of this lovely book. I've never actually done so, yet I feel as though I have trotted for miles with him knee-to-knee, stirrups clanking, watching hounds and talking horses. We haven't even met very many times, yet I count him as a terrific friend. So might you, once you've finished this book. Few people these days convey so much, so well, with the written word. Reading about David's mounted adventures is the next best thing to being in the saddle.

And if this Foreword includes as many of David's words as my own, I make no apology for it; I cannot match him. He may now have hung up his hat, but his adventures endure.

Thank you, David, so very much.

Lucy Higginson
Editor, *Horse & Hound*
December 2011

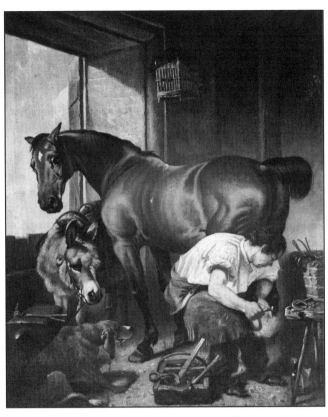

'Shoeing the Bay Mare' by James Wheeler of Bath
(after Landseer's famous painting)
© *The Holburne Museum*

Acknowledgements

Special thanks to Edmund Squibb for his help with the photographs, and to Helen Lorentzen for the cover picture of my horses waiting for their evening feed.

INTRODUCTION

Them... and us

AT LEAST twice they have been signposts at crucial turnings in my life. Ponies helped me up that tall step from boy to man; one particular horse, a great leonine Irish Draft chestnut gelding called Woody, eased me into my third career, as a hunting correspondent; others, particularly home-bred, home-broken Dandy and Bella, have brought joy and a great sense of something worthwhile done, to middle-life and to old age.

I was a timid, weakly child, useless at football, my sister being picked before me when, at our prepschool, teams were being made up. Is there any greater torture than waiting... waiting... beside the pitch or by the gymnasium wall-bars, and not being called forward, wishing you were invisible? I could never throw a cricket ball or vault a wooden horse, and my flat-footed attempts at running were a joke.

What is more I never belonged to a gang, nor ever had a 'best friend': when I had occasion for a 'Best Man'

I more or less asked the next person who came through the door.

But my first proper pony, a skewbald called Punch, taught me at the age of twelve that he and his sort would give me their company and their trust, and, what was even more important, lend me their strength, athleticism and courage. I learned from Punch, and his successors, of the endearing docility and gentleness of horses, of how, except in fear or play, they habitually discount their great strength in their dealings with puny us.

They have also taught me what I regard as two of the most important rules in life, 'to ride on a loose rein', and to trust intuition, follow my feelings, read faces rather than small print. For better or worse, horses have made me the man I am, really helped me through life. Do you wonder that I love them?

I profoundly believe that the animals that are our companions, pets and servants, be they elephants or hamsters, civilize us, make us human, teach us how to live; but for some of us, animals mean even more than that. This is the story of what horses have meant to me....

... if mere humans seem sometimes to have little more than walk-on parts in the story, you should know that I am probably the happiest married man in the world. Diana and I have, between us, four 'children', her girls and my boys, and six grandchildren at the last count. We have been married for over thirty years.

1

Shoeing the Bay Mare

WE DO well to give careful thought to the pictures that have the first say in young lives. These earliest of images stay with us, furnishing, perhaps even peopling, a growing child's expanding mind and imagination. Leastways, I have never forgotten the Landseer that hung in our nursery, redolent as it is of the smells, anvil-music and gossip of the forge, in the days before farriers took to the road.

That picture *(see page 8)* was prophetic. When, after WWII we came to live in Dorset, I and my sister Helen were to spend hours of our school holidays at our pony's, or my father's horse's head, in the smithy off Duck Street in Cerne Abbas, a good long ride over Giant's Head from home.

Our nursery, pre-war, had been in Somerset, at South Petherton, the first home that I can remember. My parents moved there in the early 1930s, not long after I was born. My father, a newly-qualified doctor, had bought the local practice. As I was to learn, as soon as we settled anywhere, even when our gypsy life started with the outbreak of war, his first concern was always to find stabling and get a horse.

He was soon hunting, with the Seavington. His scarlet coat, as my mother used to tell me every time she saw me wear it, Bernard Weatherill's journeyman measured him for, and fitted, in front of our Somerset drawing-room fire. Its label bears the date 25th June 1938. How could that young doctor, with the world opening up before him, have guessed that he had just one hunting season to enjoy before all its promise came to a sudden end? In 1938 he was 31 years old; I just five.

The old coat has not lacked use but has worn well. I still wore it, even after the wretched 'ban', when kindly so invited, for instance at our opening meet, or when hounds meet here, in our paddock, for the South Dorset's first outing in our demanding vale.

* * *

I CAN'T remember much more of my first pony, Cherrypie, than you can gather from his picture. A no-doubt naughty Shetland, he lived in a paddock across the road from our South Petherton front door. When war came all that vanished, suddenly. My father, who didn't have to, enlisted, in the Royal Army Medical Corps, sold

Cherrypie: my first pony, a Shetland

up, the house going with the practice, and our 'gypsy' life began, my mother taking rooms or renting nearby whereever he was posted.

The 'phoney war' found us in Essex, in an old millhouse, where my mother, sister and grandmother later miraculously survived a direct hit by a stray German bomb. My father built a stable with railway sleepers in the garage, got a horse over from his brother in Hampshire, and was set on hunting. But then the war got going in earnest, he was appointed Medical Officer on troopships, and spent the rest of hostilities afloat.

One writes of it lightly, but it is not difficult to imagine what it can have been like for a young mother of three children, with in due course a fourth on the way, to be snatched out of the comfortable and settled life she had married into... or indeed for the young man to have the promising world at his feet suddenly vaporise.... both uprooted and un-roofed, living in daily fear of what might happen to the other next. Truly, for them, and for all of their heroic cohort who saw the war through, making the best of it, it was a case of '*Goodbye to All That*'.

With peace, out of uniform at last, my father bought a medical practice based in the village of Buckland Newton, mid-Dorset. It was as close to our old Somerset home as professional etiquette, in those days of private practice, allowed him to 'set up his plate'.

We had hardly settled before he took himself off to Taunton market to buy himself a hunter, and, rather like beanstalk Jack, came home with two, ever hopeful that he would persuade my mother back into the saddle and into the hunting field.

He might have had a better chance of doing this if the horse he bought for her had not been a chestnut mare, who proved to have her full share of the engaging waywardness associated with that gender and that colour – I have come to love chestnut mares, but Ruby was not the best choice for a nervous and reluctant rider. My mother seldom rode and never again hunted.

Neither of his Taunton purchases turned out well: there was a lot of four-legged rubbish about in those immediate post-war years. He was not really well suited until he bought a retired steeple-chaser of great quality and considerable price called Singing Knight, which won the Hunt Race for him and, returned to a training stable, gave us all immense fun.

One of his new hunting acquaintances, the late Lady Digby, told him of a good pony looking for a new home: that is how Punch came into our lives (price £40), my sister met her future husband, Punch's previous

My sister Helen on Bob and me on Punch. Note my head-gear: health and safety hadn't been invented

owner, and I started to grow-up. I was 13 years old and the year was 1946.

* * *

ALMOST the first thing my father taught me as I learnt to ride was that, however attached to a horse I might become *emotionally*, I must never allow myself to be physically attached, by rope or leather – he didn't use the 'e' word of course, one didn't in those unenlightened days, reticence and the stiff upper lip had yet to be abolished. He particularly impressed on me never to ride in gumboots, for fear of one sticking in the stirrup, leading to being dragged should you fall, and getting your brains kicked out. As a country doctor he was no doubt speaking from experience.

The other early lesson I remember learning from him was always to stand *close* to a kicker, the damage from a mailed hoof being far greater when the horse's leg is at full stretch. This turned out to be sound advice with dangerous humans too: twice in the Army I was to find myself serving on the personal staff of notorious fire-eaters: they were much easier to manage and less dangerous close up!

Soon we were hunting, my sister and I. This was long before anyone other than farmers had lorries or trailers and petrol was anyway still rationed. Hunting meant hacking to a meet, anything up to ten miles, then sometimes much more than that home. Riding a tired pony back to its stable, perhaps in the dark, feeding it, settling it, checking that it had not 'broken out' in sweat, are among the strongest of memories of that very happy time. That, and the joys of the Pony Club, where one met *girls*!

One particular, marathon hack still lives in my memory. It was the last week of the summer holidays and I was shortly due back to school at Clifton, Helen at Roedean. We begged our reluctant father, who disliked early hours, to let us turn out for the only possible cubbing meet, at Waddock Cross, full eleven miles away by ruler on the map, nearer twenty in the saddle.

Goodness knows at what hour and in what light we set out, one of us on the treasured Punch, one on borrowed Bob; one of us managing the gates, the other leading my father's horse. The aim was if possible never to touch a road, our route being across the heart of Dorset's downland sheepwalks, by long-disused ways and tracks, now bridleways, the county's 'ghost roads' as I later learnt to call and to cherish them.

We got to that distant meet, but my father never did. As so often in his busy, devoted doctor's life, he had been 'called out'. There were of course no mobile telephones in those days, so we waited, and waited, then, guessing what had happened, rode sadly all that long way home.

SOMEHOW, I managed to get almost to the end of my schooldays without having any fixed idea as to what I was going to do next, no sense whatever of a vocation, dreading the question adults tend to ask when they can think of nothing else to say to pubescent youth.

It had been assumed that I would be a doctor, so after School Certificate, the equivalent of today's O-levels, I joined the Science stream. That this wasn't a great success you may judge from the fact that, in my Higher Certificate ('A-level') biology practical exam, I mistook the sheep's eye we were given to dissect for some sort of onion, carefully drawing and describing it as such, and scored zero marks.

Lucky chance, or, more likely, a wise guiding hand, took me into English classes in the Upper Sixth. We studied Thomas Hardy's *The Woodlanders* under a brilliant scholar, the Headmaster, and you might say that 'the dog saw the rabbit'. When my sixth form essay tutor asked me where I had *copied* something from, accusing me of plagiarism, it just started to dawn on me that I could write, and that writing might be my thing.

The other thing I have to thank my schooldays for is a lifelong love of music. A bout of rheumatic fever between schools sent me late to Clifton, my voice already breaking, but I got into the choir as a bass and can never forget the thrill of singing for our heroic one-armed Director of Music, Dr Douglas Fox. I still sing, when no one is there to listen except for my long-suffering horses, especially when I'm riding over Dungeon Hill, which stands above our house.

It was my mother who, not unintentionally I am sure, set my forward course by asking "You won't go in the Army, will you?" I had never seriously thought of it

My father on his steeple-chaser, Singing Knight, which won the Hunt Race for him

until then, and thought of nothing else thereafter. My House Tutor set the seal on it by one day asking me across the table at lunch in Big School – I can see him standing there, and hear him still – "How would you like to join a crack cavalry regiment?"

The big question, the only worry, when I later went for interview with the then-Colonel of the 13th/18th Royal Hussars (Queen Mary's Own) over lunch in the Cavalry Club, was would I need a private income, and, if so, how little could I scrape by on? The old general, a dear man who made the awesome occasion as easy as possible for an awkward youth, settled the matter by saying that so long as my father would help me out when I needed to buy a horse I could manage perfectly well on my pay.

So that is how it came about that May Day 1952 saw a very callow nineteen-year-old, boarding a train at Sherborne station, *en route* for Carlisle and his first day in the service of the young Queen, who had recently succeeded her heroic father but was not yet crowned.

2

Gone for a Soldier

IN THOSE days the only way to Sandhurst was through the ranks. We did four months 'basic training' as private soldiers, in my case, since I was headed for the Royal Armoured Corps, as a Trooper. There was, however, no danger of being mistaken for a genuine private soldier, as white stripes on the epaulettes of our battle-dress marked us out as Potential Officers, more usually referred to as "Effing POs".

It was a strange situation for a public school boy, fun in a tough sort of way, and it was no doubt very good for us to experience barrack-room life and the exigencies of canteen and cookhouse. I can never forget doing guard duty, the hell of having to keep awake and alert through a two hour 'stag', two or three times in the night. I have often doubted the wisdom of putting an end to compulsory entry through the ranks – the Army's future officers go straight to Sandhurst now.

The late Tim Forster, then heading for the Cherry-pickers, the 11th Hussars, but who was later to make a big name for himself as a racehorse trainer, was in the next bunk to me in that Carlisle barrack-room. Somehow, somewhere, he had a car. One day, scanning the racing pages of a daily newspaper he said, "I see that your father has an entry at Cheltenham, let's go and watch him run." It was an epic day: Singing Knight ran second.

* * *

MY FATHER came to visit during my first week at Sandhurst, the pretext being the Camberley Horse Show. He had a look round, and discovered stables in the grounds, at the Staff College, where a few of the senior, more leisured, officer cadets kept horses. He said, "You need a horse here. You can have Duchess. Come down and fetch her as soon as they let you out."

As those who experienced it will remember, and others may without difficulty imagine, the first term at Sandhurst is tough going; they mean to find out what you are made of, and run you off your feet. You might think that I *needed* a horse at that juncture like I needed the proverbial hole in the head, but my father's naïf intervention, inspired possibly by that benign old general's remark as to his paternal duties, was to turn out well for me.

As soon as we were granted leave-of-absence I took a train home, rode the said Duchess, a rather grumpy bay Irish mare, down to Sherborne station, where a pre-ordered box was waiting for us in a siding, and took the first of only two rail journeys with a horse I ever made.

It was a strange experience, to be alone with your horse, completely out-of-touch, a piece, as it were, on someone's board, in some distant, one hoped attentive, official's board-game; connected now to this train, now to that, now shunted into a siding, then on the move again.

Blackwater Station was in darkness when we eventually unboxed there, the lights and traffic on the A30 terrifying, something I had never experienced with a horse in hand before – I had soon quit the saddle. It was a great relief to arrive at Duchess's new home, a stall in a busy stable, and to hand her over to a man who was to become both ally and mentor, her groom and mine, a very Irish Corporal Donohoe, of the 4th/7th Royal Dragoon Guards.

* * *

"I CALL you 'Sir', and *you* call *me* 'Sir': the difference is that *you* really mean it!" was among the introductory remarks directed at us newly-arrived officer cadets by our Grenadier Guards Company Sergeant Major, a truly admirable man. It is a phrase that, suitably adapted, has often revisited the mind in my dealings with professional Hunt Servants, their old-world courtesy bartered for my profound respect. How I honour free spirits who lead hazardous outdoor lives in a world tyrannised by office folk fixated on 'elf-n-safety', and a crass polity that would shackle our every word and step, infantilise us all!

The deal with Cpl Donohoe was not dissimilar. He was the first old-fashioned cavalry Non Commissioned Officer (NCO) I ever worked closely with, and he taught me, unconsciously I'm sure, how informality, tempered with a necessary distance and mutual respect rub shoulders in the often close confines of soldiering (not least, inside the hull of a tank or armoured car).

I was not happy at all that Duchess stood in a stall, not a loose box, was desperate to have her well-exercised, daily; would somehow get on her back before first parade whenever I could, and as long as the shortening days allowed. On Wednesday and Saturday afternoons she was my escape from the dreaded treadmill of the rugger and cricket pitch.

In season we followed the Staff College Drag Hounds, out-of-season we explored the Academy's hinterland, a great stretch of empty heath and woodland called Barossa Common; it was heaven. But that was not the only pay-off on my father's inspired contribution to my eighteen months at the Royal Military Academy.

I have no doubt at all that regularly hacking home from an afternoon with the Drag Hounds in the company of Sandhurst's Commandant, a terrifying major-general, did me no harm at all, and contributed to his mentioning my name in his final address to us all, before announcing that the runner-up for the Sword of Honour was someone else! However, I passed-out high enough to get into the regiment of my choice, which was all that really mattered.

* * *

OF ALL the departures and new beginnings in a soldier's life none surely can compare with when he first joins his regiment. Mine was stationed outside a small north German town called Wolfenbüttel. The year was 1954, we were still, in effect, part of an occupying army, the war a recent memory, etched on the tunic breasts of many of my seniors.

One benefit of this was that there were horses to be had, good horses, that had been 'liberated', by a British cavalry general nine years before, from the Wehrmacht stud at nearby Mecklenhorst. They were not supposed to be taken out of the country when their owners were posted, and must only change hands for a standard price of about £15.

So my father got off lightly with this my first purchase, his son mounted out of battlefield loot. To reduce the burden of my monthly stable bill, I shared ownership with a brother officer. The horse in question was a mare of the Trakehner, that is to say of an East Prussian/Polish breed, called Fortuna.

I never rode a tougher, braver, more loveable horse; we had endless fun together in the show jumping and cross-country events that peppered the summer calendar in those light-hearted days. She was almost never lame, and I don't remember her ever saying "No!": she did the world of good to my confidence, continuing where Punch had left off, and making up for the slightly iffy moments I had sometimes had with grumpy Duchess following the Sandhurst Drag Hounds.

* * *

HOW can I convey to you, what it was like to join the regiment that was to be my second family and home for the next twenty years? I truly believe that there is nothing quite to compare with the character of a good British regiment, its genius for making the best of the human material that comes its way.

Being by nature solitary and bookish, I was quite unsuited to the gregarious *milieu* that I had so blindly drifted into. Mess life, with its late hours, horseplay and all but compulsory jollity, was inimical to me, and was to remain so throughout all my service. But my regiment took me to its heart, and I was in due course, for three wonderful years, entrusted with its command, than which I believe there is no finer thing in the whole world of work for a man to do – to command a regiment in the British Army.

If my heart was in the regimental stables, as a Troop Leader the vehicle park was my place of work. We were a reconnaissance regiment, that is to say we were equipped with ancient Daimler armoured cars. My troop had a pair of the beastly things, with their horrible ear-splitting two-pounder guns, and a further pair of open scout cars that we called dingoes. My command comprised about a dozen men.

I was of course a boy amongst those men. It was a sort of two-way paternalism, each having something to offer the other, the classic situation in which a subaltern fresh out of Sandhurst finds himself. Based on an ancient class and education system, and no doubt abhorrent to all right-minded – left-minded? – progressive folk, it works extremely well in most cases.

Command at that level is a greenhouse where young men mature rapidly and visibly: when I myself came to command a squadron it was pleasure to me to see in my young Troop Leaders how soon a boy learnt a man's ability to put himself in others' shoes, to think of nothing before his soldiers' welfare. It is also an anvil on which a young man is shaped, tempered, and made fit for use.

Fortuna, my share of World War II booty.
I never rode a tougher, braver, more
loveable horse

3

Letters Home

THE STORY of the next few years or so is told in the letters I sent home Sunday by Sunday, sometimes oftener, which we found in a tin box in the attic when, just across the threshold of the present century and a month short of her 93rd birthday, over thirty years a widow, my mother died.

The Sunday-letter habit, learned by the prep-school boy, finally faltered, then petered out, in the married man. But there are some hundreds of them, starting in a characterless, barely legible scrawl (what in the family we called a 'spider's Derby', which had the advantage of concealing my then and still now total inability to spell) and ending in the rather laboured broad-nibbed italic script that I copied from my father's hand and still attempt today.

I am not so foolish as to suppose that my old letters are of any interest now to anybody other than their writer. But perhaps a few selected brush-strokes from them may help you picture the sort of life a rather over-serious, horse-mad young soldier led in those so different, distant days.

The first batch, over eighty scrawls, each of between one and six pages, takes us from when I first joined my regiment in 1954, the centenary year of the Battle of Balaklava and the Charge of the Light Brigade, a proud memory in my new family, to a point two-and-a-half years later when I was, for the first time posted home.

Fortuna features every time. In fact the letters are almost more her biography than mine. Typically, she *jumped marvellously… is full of bounce… jumped like a dream…. has mastered the catch on the door of her box….* and so on. One six-pager written to my father in October 1955, while mother was in hospital, tells of how I shamelessly overdrew on her courage and patience, entering her in five different events at one horse-show, took a fall, actually got her refusing, almost soured her off.

I was learning: she was teaching. Incurably hard-mouthed, she taught me to guide, trust, and talk to her, rather than fight her – an invaluable lesson, horses being so much stronger than we are – but perhaps best of all the qualities of that tough little mare was that she

*Fortuna show jumping: I don't remember
her ever saying "No!"*

was forgiving. Throughout all, we remained the best of friends. I longed to bring her home with me, but was not allowed to, and had to sell her on to a brother officer when the time came to leave.

Of course life wasn't all riding and horse-shows. The great thing as a young officer was to keep your men busy, challenged and interested. That meant getting out of barracks with them, and as often as possible; we were continually in the field. And, if I was lucky in my first horse, I was even luckier in my first Commanding Officer. An Irish Baronet with a gallantry medal, a DSO, a man of character and a brilliant horseman, he was a god to me. Reading between the lines of my letters home it is evident that he also approved of me, if not of my horsemanship.

We rode a lot together. He would lend me his second horse for competitive riding on the rare occasions Fortuna was off work; but he sent me home to do riding school with the Household Cavalry at Windsor, an unforgettable experience. He also sent me on a week's course to Paris, officially to learn about NATO, but I fancy he had other gaps in my education in mind (I had been seen polishing off the *Times* crossword puzzle, a knack learnt as a schoolboy: "If we don't watch out, that young fellow will be writing bloody poetry next!").

Finally, a badge of trust, he sent me to be the Regiment's representative on the staff of what was then called the Boys' Squadron, at Bovington, barely twenty miles from home.

* * *

BOVINGTON was too good to last, but in fact something even better came my way. I had barely bought myself a horse, not least as a means of transport for the four hour ride between work and home – the Boys' Squadron had school holidays – had him going to my satisfaction, including with hounds, when a summons came to re-join my old squadron, which had been detached to Aden at short notice, and on active service.

Two memories survive from that brief home interlude. Regularly traversing the county, almost its full depth from north to south and vice-versa, I became fascinated with Dorset's old abandoned roads and tracks, and studied their history, learnt to love and value them. I think of that time as being one of the happiest I can remember. I loved the work, but spent ages in the saddle, with just the company of my horse, escaping the embarrassments and puzzles of that so over-rated thing called youth. That, and, in my Spring holiday, riding with my father the hundred miles to Exmoor, stopping two nights en-route each way, our horses over-nighting in pub orchards. It was an unforgettable experience, and included my first day stag-hunting.

Tara, as my horse was called, was near clean-bred, purchased with point-to-pointing in mind. I found him down west, can't remember where, but I do remember what decided me to buy him. I'd seen him, ridden him of course, liked him, but come home a-dither, worried about his price, and where the money would come from.

That evening, sitting with my parents in the drawing-room, listening to music as was their way, they had Elgar's *Enigma Variations* on the turntable. *Nimrod* settled the matter for me, such a stirring, decisive tune. I left the room: telephoned: bought the horse on the never-

*Tara, bred for point-to-pointing and bought
with borrowed funds*

never. There was a regimental fund that we officers all subscribed to that advanced money on easy repayment terms for just such emergencies.

Tara later duly won a point-to-point for his next owner, whilst I found myself, on my 25th birthday, a very temporary captain, commanding all the soldiers that the British Army had deployed at that time in distant Oman! It was real *Boys Own* soldiering. I had a half-squadron of two troops, and we were detached twelve hundred miles away from my boss in Aden, to whom I reported daily on the radio.

It was the only time in my career, as far as I know, that I was ever shot at, or was in anything approaching a war. After less than a year of that I found myself pitchforked into quite another sort of soldiering, in Malaya, learning to play polo, which was to become an obsession for the next twenty years, and riding in my first ever race. We played polo off discarded racehorses, which we occasionally returned to the track to ride in amateur races.

* * *

"I AM now running the stables" a letter from Ipoh of October 1958 tells, *"we have bought five ponies.... It is marvellous to get on a horse again"*. The following month, writing from hospital, badly shaken and somewhat cut about by a car crash, *"we played our first game of polo on Monday, three a-side. I can't tell you what fun it was. I aim to be riding again by the end of this week"*.

Then, two weeks later, *"I am riding a horse called Sovereign at present, he is a gift from one of the racing stables... bought as a yearling by the Regent of Johore for three thousand pounds, he won the Gold Cup here and holds the course record... raced as a two-year-old he has become sour.... I hope to turn him into a polo pony"*.

But, on the day before we were due to play our first proper match *"I had a most unfortunate fall... Sovereign was frightened by a lorry in the road, he reared and fell backwards onto me, and then rolled on me. How I escaped serious injury was a miracle... he has lost a lot of skin but is not lame... I am alright now, and was able to play in the match next day... we players were all introduced to the Sultan of Perak... he is a dear old man... we are now switched off polo to racing.... I have two rides for most Saturdays"...* and so on!

* * *

AGAIN, I was to find myself unexpectedly on the move. The Regiment had to provide an adjutant for The Queen's Own Yorkshire Yeomanry, our affiliated Territorial Army regiment. Suddenly I was on my way to enjoying three seasons in a hunting heaven. For, if fellow Jane Austen addicts will forgive me, it is surely a truth universally acknowledged that a young bachelor on the loose in a sporting county must be in need of rides. I was almost overwhelmed, hunting sometimes as often as four days a week, seldom less than two and had at one time no fewer than three horses in my stable.

Perhaps it will come as no surprise to you to learn that I left Yorkshire, to join the staff at Sandhurst, an engaged man. Also wiser. I had found out the hard way that point-to-pointing was not for me, I just did not have the athleticism or judgement for it and must have been a menace to my fellow jockeys. Such as it is, my horsemanship is of a quiet sort, relying, I like to think, much more on empathy and mutual trust than on any formal skill.

In six outings over two seasons I finished only once, fell four times, once ending up in hospital with a fractured humerus, which still from time to time reminds me of the occasion; and of the rather dodgy mare involved, Easterly Breeze, my first ride over fences. Her owner had, in a prophetic phrase, asked me if I cared to 'chance my arm' racing his difficult young horse.

I was not cut out for point-to-pointing, fell four times in six outings and Easterly Breeze helped me fracture my arm

JUST a few more 'brush-strokes' and we will shut the lid on that old tin box of my mother's, as the letter-writing habit faded…

York, January 31ˢᵗ 1960 *"… had wonderful day's hunting on Monday… the young horse went really well. I'm hunting her again tomorrow and have been exercising her all week… she's full sister to Easter Breeze, that won the Grand Military last year… it's a strange thing, but she goes for me very well, but won't behave for others… just one of those odd things, I hope it lasts… the wife of one of the Middleton Joint Masters is sending me a young horse tomorrow, to make for her. It should be rather fun…."* Work gets a mention, as a tax-payer you will no doubt be glad to learn, then the letter ends… *"it's been a full week."*

York again, April 10ᵗʰ, *"… we had a satisfactory* (first) *outing yesterday… pulled up a mile from home… the ride was a great thrill. On Friday went to the p-to-p ball, which was fun… went to a cocktail party after the races and then to a dance at Barnard Castle… got back at 7am this morning… went to the St Matthew Passion in the Minster this afternoon, it was beautifully done. Easterly Breeze is quite well today, I'm very stiff".*

The reference to the Bach is timely. For all the horsy and other excitements in my young life, the pull of music never slackened, and has stayed with me, a constant joy. The other constant theme in my letters home was thanks for the books, which throughout my bachelor soldiering, my father regularly mailed me. He took a very close interest in my reading; it has been the indispensable basis of my writing; I can never adequately honour his memory for it.

A fortnight later... *"We had a rather unfortunate outing... fell at the second fence. Yesterday... did better... but.... She made a mistake five from home and fell. We were well set for a place... I think we really may do something next time, she gets a bit close to her fences...*

A cracker of a thoroughbred: Jungle Boy and I really bonded

I hope she will have learnt from her fall yesterday...." You
know the rest.

One of the least likeable characteristics of that
mare was that she couldn't be mounted in the parade
ring, and if you tried, she would rear straight up, perpendicular. By special agreement with the stewards, her
owner having pull, I was always thrown into the saddle
on the move as we quit the ring for the start: not an ideal
routine for the greenest of jockeys. By next season I had
my own point-to-pointer, a cracker of a thoroughbred
hunter called Jungle Boy that I really bonded with, but
we didn't do much better.

*On the parade
ground with
Farouk*

After Sandhurst, and a year as a student at the Staff College, hunting occasionally with the Drag again, I returned to be Adjutant of my own regiment, when, as well as playing polo madly (and badly – no better than my racing if the truth be told, but I adored it, thought of little else for twenty years) I had the use of a Government range patrol horse, a massive Hanoverian called Farouk.

We did a lot together, Farouk and I, for he was a fearless jumper and nothing fazed him. But my proudest memory is of riding him, when, as was my duty as Adjutant, I put the Regiment through its paces on the drill square.

* * *

THE next ten years or so after the last letter quoted were full of four-legged-friends, too many to name here, if not to remember. Polo, which flourished in Germany, was the big thing; and I hunted when the occasional home posting made that possible, on a big clumsy horse called Casper, not one of my most inspired purchases. He did his best to kill me by somersaulting over a badly misjudged iron gate. Then I finished regimental service, handing over command to the good friend who had, all those years before, shared Fortuna with me.

At last, in 1987, with very mixed feelings, I quit the Army, it having finally surrendered in what had been a long tug-o-war with the Dorset home, which had been mine since my father's tragically early death.

So much for my Sunday letters. When my mother died, it chanced that my wife Diana was away and I was on my own. Returning in the evening to an empty house so full of memories of my mother, before inevitably picking up the telephone and with it the burdens of bereavement, re-engaging with the family and the outside world at one of the most sorrowful moments in my life, I could think of nothing better than, for a short while, to keep company with the horses, who are so companionable, contented, confiding and reassuring, especially when they are at grass.

Casper, a big, clumsy horse who did his best to kill me by somersaulting over a badly misjudged iron gate

4

Coming Home:
Daisy and Woody

FIRST impressions go a long way with me. It's all of thirty years ago, but I can never forget when I first met Daisy. It was over the door of her loose-box at an Armed Services saddle-club in Germany. She had just arrived, a few hours before, from England. As we were to learn, she never travelled easily, always took ages to settle in new places: now she was obviously in a mega tizz, you could see it in her eye. But she came to me, seemingly to be comforted, to be reassured. Something clicked; and you might say that we never looked back.

She was a six-year-old, Irish bred, a bay Irish Draft/Thoroughbred cross, sixteen-and-a-half hands, very typical hunter-type. She had presence, was a good-looker, as people often told me, but was never going to win a point-to-point. The Saddle Club, of which I was the Chairman, had bought her in the hope that she

Daisy with her first foal Dandy

would make our name in the hunter-trials and events that still filled the summer calendar in those pre-Iraq, pre-Afghanistan, carefree soldiering days.

She didn't: our investment was a total failure! For one thing she couldn't eat normal dry hay, couldn't be bedded on straw, coughed at the slightest excuse – in due course we found that wood-chip bedding and *Horsehage* took care of that. Worse, she just could not settle happily to the life of a saddle-club 'tart' with every Tom, Dick and Harriet riding her.

Very nervous and cranky by nature, cold-backed amongst other things – she once sat down, literally, like a circus horse, when I climbed into the plate – she scared the pants off just about everybody who rode her, including such VIPs as the Air Marshal's wife, etc etc. It soon became apparent that she was a one-man-horse – and that lucky man was me.

When we were posted home, to sighs of relief all round we purchased Daisy, the best money I ever spent, and brought her back to England with us. That was when, for the first time since leaving home for the Army, I found myself once again my own groom; and was reminded, not just of the hard manual work that I had skipped, but, more to the point, of what I had missed, what are perhaps the chief pleasures and intimacies of horse-ownership.

We spent a year on Old Sarum airfield in Wiltshire, where (probably quite illegally) I built a lean-to stable for her on the end of our married quarter. Of an evening, we could actually hear her through the wall of our sitting room. It was almost as if she was living with us. Then, bliss, no doubt through some cock-up in the Ministry of Defence, my last army posting was one that enabled us to live at my old Dorset home, and Daisy had the run of the stables and paddocks I had known and loved since a boy.

* * *

IT was an exciting moment, taking Daisy hunting for the first time. I had no doubt that she had seen hounds during her Irish 'childhood', and I had done a little jumping on her here and there, just to make sure that she was not averse to leaving the ground. She had seemed willing enough, if not especially bold, but what sort of a hunter would she make? I had no idea.

In South Dorset's downland with its timber fences she turned out to be a star. It was not just that she seemed to love popping over rails – if there were any sort of queue she would be revving up, saying, "Can we go please? Can we go PLEASE... NOW!?" – but she was so neat and nimble with it. Soon she had a following: people knew her for a sound pilot, knew that her rather matronly back-end was a good one to follow.

One particular moment sticks in the mind. We had met down by the sea at Holworth, gorgeous, spectacular

David on Daisy

country to follow hounds in. A rather tall, narrow stile hove into view, designed for rambling not for jumping, profoundly uninviting. Would she show the way? I can see her front hooves now, ever so neatly tucked up beside her shoulder in that confined space, almost seem to hear her say "Easy-peasy!"

If she was a treasure in the downland, the demanding Tuesday vale country round home told another story. Her paces being a bit pony-like, she just lacked the scope for the big fly fences, and did not fancy them; they frightened her. Robin Gundry had our hounds then, and his wife Helen kindly rode Daisy for me in the vale one day, and gave her top rating. But Daisy and I just didn't combine well in the vale – draw your own conclusions!

One memorable day we didn't quite make it over one of the famous Pulham hedges, and ended up spread-eagled on the top of it, stuck. I can't remember exactly how we extricated ourselves. It was the nearest thing to a fall she ever gave me out hunting, but it wasn't a fall really, more of a scramble down. That evening, in my bath, I decided that I must get a proper vale horse – enter the great Woody.

It was some years after that that we decided to breed from Daisy. We took her down to the Brendons, to Diana Scott's Ben Fairie, the famous eventing sire. She took, but we lost that foal on the journey back. As I told you, and we should have remembered, she travelled badly.

Next year we took her to 'the boy next door', Pablond, at Pitt's Farm Stud, just a short walk away, actually in our own parish.

Dandy was born next year and following that Bella – Dandelion and Bluebell if we are being formal. Daisy, Dandelion, Bluebell... *geddit*?

She dropped Dandy, who was to grow up to be the spitting image of her, one magic summer afternoon, in our paddock, the whole village watching.

Bella, I found one morning a year later, just for the first time struggling to her feet, in the stable when I went to give her mother an early breakfast. When I told Diana that we had a chestnut filly she burst into prophetic tears; a chestnut mare with Daisy's tricky DNA was the one thing we dreaded.

I think that the best way to describe Daisy's life with us, once she had decided it was 'home', had settled into hunting and motherhood, is to say that, as in fairy stories, she lived happily ever after. She managed to get over her fear of strangers riding her, especially if they were non-threatening females. My nieces used to ride her when they came down to hunt in their school holidays. A neighbour's daughter used to ride her at exercise, and in fact took her down to the Cotley country for her last hunting season, before she came home to retire. But, of course, there was, however distant, always that dreaded end in sight.

I HATE playing God with animals. But when you take on responsibility for a dog, horse, hamster or whatever, you overdraw on happiness. Sooner or later the day comes when the account has to be squared, the debt is called in – it is as well to be prepared.

On a very cold morning late one January, when I was due to be hunting the best part of 100 miles away on Dartmoor, and was actually walking to the car, dressed for work, a kind call from the huntsman forestalled me. Contrary to forecast, the moor was frozen solid. There was no prospect whatever of those hounds being taken out that day.

I had already visited the outside horses, and Daisy seemed unwilling to move. For some days, instead of coming for her meals, she'd had to be escorted to the hayrack. I would walk out to wherever dawn or dusk found her, say, "Come on old girl", and she would plod confidingly beside me to the shelter, where I would, if necessary, elbow myself in to make a space for her, to ensure that she got her fair share of grub.

But on that morning she just would not budge. I took hay to her, noting that she would probably need water to be taken to her later. When I told Diana we both shook our heads. There was no spare stable for her, and what was the point anyway of bringing her inside? We both knew that at last her time had come, and what needed to be done.

By chance, the South Dorset were meeting next door that same morning. I went round on foot, meaning to speak to our then kennel huntsman, David Boulter. David rode short, jockey-style almost, and he was on an enormous grey – I found myself addressing the toe of his polished boot. With the old-fashioned courtesy that is the proud badge of hunt service, and owes nothing whatever to servility, he bent down and replied quietly to my query. "Is it old Daisy? Yes, sir, bring her along tomorrow morning." The die was cast.

I left that meet feeling desperate, with a palpable constriction in my chest: horrified at what I had committed myself to, and wondering how on earth I was going to follow through. Kept myself busy, away from home all day, trying to come to terms with what had totally surprised me. When it came to the point, I could hardly bear to think of parting with Daisy.

I deplore sentimentality over animals, it is the cause of so many of our present problems: look where it has got us with hunting – and badgers. But through three-quarters of her life, and quite a chunk of mine, Daisy and I had spent weeks, months, if you were to tot it up, in each other's exclusive company. However unintelligent in our terms – they cannot after all fly to the moon, wage wars, or organize concentration camps – horses forget nothing, and give their trust discerningly; there was a bond between us, that shy, nervous mare and me, as witnessed by the way she would walk beside me to her hay. But, by the end of an unhappy day, my head had explained to my heart where duty lay.

So Daisy's last day came. She boxed easily, thinking, no doubt, that she was going hunting. We drove the 20 miles to the kennels, and I left her, stabled between two hunt horses, alert, interested in her neighbours, and aware of the smell and occasional sound of hounds.

With David's help I put some borrowed clothing on her, careful not to meet his eye, gave her one last Judas hug, scooped up our rug and head-collar, ran for it, and drove blindly home, the brigadier all but blubbing like a baby.

* * *

I FIRST met Woody in the pages of *Horse & Hound*, giving the then-Editor Michael Clayton a wonderful ride with the Galway Blazers. There was one of Jim Meads' inimitable pictures, and I thought "That could be just the horse for me!" If you want to follow hounds in the South Dorset's famous Tuesday country, you've just got to have a really bold, strong, athletic horse, which can cope with the deep clay and big fly fences.

Next heard of, Woody was in Barbara Rich's Thorpe Satchville yard, showing off his paces in the Quorn country. Diana, also horse-hunting on her own

*Woody: for the South Dorset's famous Tuesday country,
you've just got to have a really bold, strong, athletic horse,
which can cope with the deep clay and big fly fences*

account, saw him and came home full of his praises. I immediately took a day off work, went up there, rode him and bought him. Barbara's head lad showed him off to me, then I climbed on board and it was a case of 'love at first sit'. He stepped off ever so boldly, just the way I like a horse to, and we jumped something – but I already knew. My chequebook was in my hand when we got back to Barbara's kitchen to talk business. I didn't even get him vetted. Who wants to be told that you can't have the horse that you have set your heart on?

Woody made his mark immediately on arrival, here at his new home. I was away at work in Taunton, where I ran a charity for people with addiction problems, but as Diana was leading him out across the lane to our meadow he spotted Daisy and jumped the gate to join her whilst Diana was still struggling with the latch. It's a full-sized, no-nonsense, five-bar gate, hung well clear of the ground. It was a good start.

He was a great escape artist: I had to re-fence every stitch of our land for his benefit. I can still see him now, jumping the big hedge and ditch out of our home paddock, seemingly to join me in the lane beyond. He liked human company which was one of the many loveable things about him.

A giant, chestnut, Irish Draft, all of seventeen-and-a-half hands, Woody was by King of Diamonds, and five-years-old when he first came to us. Like so many big horses, he had done a bit too much whilst 'in the shop window' when still a growing youngster, something that he and I were to pay for later. In fact it was Woody's comparatively short working life, shortened by navicular disease, that decided us to have a go at breeding and gently bringing-on our own hunters.

My new mount was soon making friends all round. He had a striking 'presence': you couldn't miss him, and he was a good one to follow across country. As soon as he saw a fence, he just wanted to be the other side; I would merely let him get on with it; it's a question really of who was the boss. I used to say that I took all the important decisions: which days we would hunt, who with, what coat to wear, when we should go home and so on; whilst he did the detailed, nitty-gritty stuff. I did the strategy, he the tactics.

You never know what's around the next corner, and what I didn't know, and couldn't possibly have guessed, when I took that impulsive journey to Thorpe Satchville almost a quarter-of-a-century ago, was that I was turning a corner in my life. Woody was to prove my passport into what I call the 'Chocolate Factory' my third career, as a Hunting Correspondent, or 'crime reporter' if you will. But for him, I would never have had the confidence to have embarked on it. As it was, I turned the offer down when it was first made to me by the then-Editor of *Country Life*.

Luckily, he came back to me, asked me a second time. Hounds were meeting here in our paddock the following week for their first vale day of the 91/92 season, and I thought, "Woody will look after me, I'll give it a whirl." You can guess the rest of the story.

What you can't guess is how lucky I was that first day. By pure good fortune, there were no heroics involved. We were the sole survivors of a field of forty at the end of a short but thrilling run, ending up completely alone with Edward Knowles and his hounds.

Our second outing brought another adventure, but of quite a different sort. It was that thing I have learnt to dread, a blank day, with four enormous staring white blank pages to be filled, somehow. As luck would have it – that word *luck* again, you need it in my trade – the Seavington had met at Cricket St Thomas, with its famous wildlife park. Hacking back for tea, wondering what on earth I was going to write about, we had the good fortune to meet a party of three elephants, one of which trumpeted a greeting. Woody, usually so imperturbable except with pigs, made off at speed, hysterical: but I had my story.

Woody carried me for sixteen of getting on for a century and a half of 'work' outings. I always used him for local packs, but also went as far afield as the Hampshire, the Berkeley and the Mendip Farmers with him. He never let me down in strange countries, or looked like doing so, but I soon learnt the wisdom of riding a locally-footed horse…. and the great advantage of not having a horse to get home and put to bed when you have a tight deadline to meet, an article struggling to get out of your head, and the urgent need to get scribbling.

Only once, in all our time together, did he stop with me, and that was on a South Dorset Tuesday, at some simple iron railings jumping into Great Wootton Wood on Dungeon, the hill behind this house. It told me immediately what we already were beginning to suspect, that he was 'feeling his feet', and that we were at the beginning of the end of Woody's warrior days.

Butazolidin was prescribed, and I hunted him happily on it, on an increasing dose, and with a sterner bit, an Army Reversible, for some seasons. Properly known as the angle-cheek Pelham, it's the bit you see in the mouths of household cavalry troop horses on state occasions: reversed it is very severe and only permitted for use in that mode by the experts, the 'rough riders'.

'Bute' seemed to render my gentle giant both deaf and numb, deaf to *my* voice that is and I have always ridden largely by voice. When *hounds* were speaking, communications between bridge and engine-room sometimes completely failed. I might as well have not been there.

The only fall he ever gave me was out with the Blackmore & Sparkford Vale, when, completely out of control, he lost his footing on one of those big concrete drains they put in culverts; I call them elephant's table-napkin rings. We were both injured, he in the shoulder, I in my ribs (I daren't laugh for a month) and in my pride, but luckily it was our last engagement of the season, and we both soon recovered.

As we limped painfully away from the scene, another but rather different hard-mouthed creature, one of the Blackmore Vale ladies, an old hand and an old friend, said, "It's your own silly, bloody fault, hunting a big horse like that on bute!"

We had a lot of fun together team chasing, in the early days, before he got to be 'footy', and actually brought home a couple of prizes. One particular event I remember was the Taunton Vale's team chase, behind

Diana and David on The Bean and Woody

Ilminster. As you turned for home there was a biggish downhill drop, the sort of thing Woody made nothing of, but I can't forget soaring over it.

For a big horse he had a great turn of speed, and was nimble with it. When *Country Life* staged a team-chase on the Balding gallops, by Watership Down, one of our team fell, horse and all, right under his feet on landing. He didn't touch either of them, I'll never know how. We won an umbrella that day, Woody and I, and I still use it!

I longed to visit Woody in retirement when he joined a herd of retirees in the Bicester country. I was so grateful to find an 'old people's home' for him – but somehow in a busy life I never could find time to go and see him, and now it's too late. Aged 28 or thereabout, he and his old, inseparable stable-mate, Diana's vale horse The Bean, 'went on', together, just a month or so before I last enquired of them.

Horses don't rely on that poor thing we humans call a memory, I'm convinced they forget nothing. I still dream of him, in the imaginary last encounter that sadly never happened, looking up from grazing, quitting his companions, and, with a low whicker, walking towards me as he always used to. Dear Woody, he was my horse of a lifetime. I owe him so much. I will never forget him.

5

Grow your Own:
Dandelion & Bluebell

ARTHUR Ransome warns us in his autobiography of
the un-wisdom of trying to design and build your own
boat: "Leave it to the experts" seems to be the tenor of
his advice. Much the same might be said of attempting
to breed your own horses; breeding is a lottery, better
surely to buy exactly what you want than take a shot in
the dark?

But, if this chapter seems to be something of a
cautionary tale – neither of Daisy's foals turned out to be
exactly what we dreamt of – the joy and satisfaction that
their two lives have brought into ours has been an experience that I would not have missed for the world. Getting
them going under the saddle, from scratch, is something
that I look back on as one of the few worthwhile achieve-
ments in an otherwise frivolous life.

"If in doubt go for it", would be *my* advice to anyone thinking of doing what we did, breeding from a favourite mare.

* * *

DANDY was born in the late spring of 1991. This turned out to be a lucky chance for me as the story of his arrival gave me just what I needed for the first article I ever wrote, the diary page in *Country Life* that I was to write every six weeks for the next twelve years. My elder step-daughter, Melanie, fairy godmother and midwife to my journalism, had tipped me off that they were looking for a new diarist. For the first, and last, time I sent an editor an un-solicited piece of writing – I never write except to a commission. Here is the gist of Dandy's birth announcement…..

"Daisy surprised us all, at about supper time one Saturday evening, before being brought in for the night. She started pawing the ground, lying down and getting up again, generally indicating that her time had come.

It was all over in an hour, but not before her fan club had gathered. Her pregnancy had been a matter of note and frequent kind inquiry locally. Alert eyes across the lane had seen what we had seen, and the whole village, or so it seemed, turned out to witness what must be one of the rarest of countryside sights.

With really no problem she produced a fine, large colt foal. Another hour saw him on his feet, to a muted cheer from the orchestra stalls behind the hedge where a debate had already started as to what he should be called. By the time he was being carried to the privacy of the stable it was a settled thing that Daisy's colt was to be Dandelion: this was duly announced from the pulpit in church the following morning, for the benefit of those who had not been present at the birth."

A rather stroppy youngster, Dandy was gelded early; we backed him when he was two years old. Having just turned sixty, and never having backed a horse before, I approached this operation with some trepidation. I need not have done, because it turned out to be a happy anti-climax.

We had of course handled him in every possible way short of actually mounting him, since birth. When I at last ventured into the saddle he merely looked round as if to ask "What *are* you doing up there?" and started to nibble the toe of my boot – he's a great nibbler, likes to test everything gently with his teeth.

He once picked up my diminutive mother-in-law by the collar of her coat, before carefully replacing her on the ground. Backing Bella a year later was to prove a similar non-event: I just climbed on board and rode her down to the village Post Office and back.

Dandy took to hunting well, like his mother, and

proved a good performer in our downland country with its mostly straightforward timber fences, but like her also he was no horse for the vale with its big hedges and deep going. At any rate he was not the right horse for *me* to ride in the vale.

I used to say that Daisy was a touch 'chicken' and that she had a barnyard fowl outcross somewhere in her ancestry. She had evidently passed this trait on to her son. Both were excellent rides so long as you did not over-face them – neither had the boldness that *this* chicken needed to get smoothly across our Tuesday country.

When I started my travels as a hunting correspondent I was usually careful where I took Dandy, although his first outing was with the Blackmore & Sparkford Vale, possibly the wettest, stormiest day's hunting I have ever experienced. I see that I told *Horse & Hound* readers that "Dandy turned up trumps, but it was largely thanks to the weather that we got away with it." In nine such outings he never stopped at a fence, never let me down: the only two falls he ever gave me, both 'hospital jobs' were both 'off duty'.

* * *

"COME on Dandikins, stir yourself!" I said into his nearest ear. I couldn't bear the thought that my old friend of so many years was dead. He had 'lost' both front feet into a rabbit hole when we were cantering a headland up above Sydling St Nicholas, bunking off church one Sunday morning, did a cartwheel, and landed squarely on top of me.

I was completely trapped, the lower half of my body under the smooth of his broad shoulder, luckily for me clear of the saddle. I could so easily have been killed outright, but in fact, at the time, had no pain: I'm told it can be like that being shot. The situation seemed comic, more than anything, except that Dandy was motionless, a dead weight. I thought that he had broken his back.

Luckily he paid no attention to my entreaties, for, when he did recover from being merely winded, his wild struggles to regain his mailed feet must surely have done for me. I had been pulled clear by then. Whilst *he* wandered quietly off to graze, unable to stand *I* lay in the sun, enjoyed the accusing sound of Sydling's church bells, and strained my ears for the usually unwelcome din of an approaching helicopter.

I found myself out of the saddle for five long months whilst my pelvis mended: Dandy was never quite the same horse again. We did a little hunting, but he seldom felt entirely sound or happy in his back.

He is now retired, although I did ride him briefly the other morning, after an interval of two years, just to spite his naughty sister who chose not to be caught – "Not to-day thank you!" she seemed to say to me, as if I were the milkman. I keep meaning to save Dandy's winter keep and 'send him on', but can't quite bring myself to do it, or bear the thought of parting him from his sister.

* * *

BELLA'S birth was a strictly private affair. Early one morning I found her struggling to her feet for the first time in Woody's old outsize loose box, which Bella now shares with her brother when we have them both in together. I have already told you how Diana received the news that we had a chestnut filly.

In fact Bella was to prove to be both a disaster and a delight, a useless hunter, but a wonderfully lively hack – you should just see how she steps away from the mounting block, game for anything, longing to see what's around the next corner. She is as bright a ride as any horse I ever sat on, and is an adorable pet.

I call her a useless hunter because you never really know what scatty thing she might do next, especially if jumping should be involved – she once knelt as if in prayer on top of a small bank: also she gets very over-excited in close company, is inclined to kick. I did twice take her on work outings, on the first occasion, in desperation, having nothing else to ride.

I see that the note of that day in my hunting log is decorated with an exclamation mark: here is how

I wrote of her… "The little horse I was on, Bella, is as green as a pea, a younger sister to Dandy, who went down with pneumonia after the Blackmore & Sparkford Vale torrential opening day, and has been wrong ever since. She had her longest day yet with hounds." That, writing in December of 1998, I called a near fully-grown sixteen-plus hand horse 'little' tells you how I thought and still think of Bella; it's ridiculous I know, but she's my 'baby'.

David on Daisy, Bella and Dandelion's mother,
exercising a quarter horse

The following month I was able to take both her and her brother to the New Forest… "I rode Dandy, and a friend's daughter, on the last day before returning for the spring term to Marlborough, rode his sister Bella.

These two horses have such a strong pair-bond that they are better hunted separately; their sibling loyalty must have been a touching sight to witness and Charlotte and I were nearly joined at the knee by the day's end. In fact it was a very happy day, and, with the trappy going, extremely educational for our two youngsters."

* * *

BELLA and I really became best pals following a disaster on the day of the solar eclipse in August 1999. For some reason, my inattention no doubt, brought on by all the endless blather and hype about the eclipse on the wireless, I had got it into my head that we were in for a period of total daytime darkness.

With this in mind, we rushed the horses out with a view to getting them exercised before stabling them safely in time for the expected and perhaps panic-inducing 'lights out' that never happened, and was never going to happen. With Diana on board, shying from a dog, Bella fell in the road, skinning both knees badly. They looked like nothing so much as a pair of bleeding eye sockets, a horrible sight, and they are still scarred.

The upshot was that we had her cooped up on box-rest for an age. I was her nurse, and had for a time to inject her daily. Her brother, so gentle in every other way, shares my hate of needles and actually shows his heels to any approaching hypodermic. Bella by contrast was utterly trusting of my ministrations, so that I found that I could do anything with her, didn't even need to tie her up. I think that that was when and why I fell in love with her: Jane Austen says something in one of her wonderful novels about how attractive it can be when someone seems to like you.

She just has one annoying habit, she knows I hate it, but nothing I do or say will make her mend her ways: she pushes me around with her nose as if I were the foal she never had. Seeming to choose her moment, she often catches me off balance, once pitching me headfirst into a bramble bush when I was reaching into it for a scrap of roadside litter. I suppose that I ought to regard her motherly attentions as a compliment.

More than any other horse that I can remember riding, Bella gives me the feeling that she is glad to have me in the saddle, that I'm part of the fun as she strides generously forward to see what is around the next corner, or over the next crest. This is especially true when we are romping over Dungeon Hill. She is not the sort of horse you would let *anybody* ride.

She is mildly alarming, but only if you don't know her ways, her paces being a touch extravagant, and, although I swear she would pass a London bus in one of our narrow lanes without twitching a whisker, she takes fright at the most ridiculous things, such as if a gnat should happen to clear its throat in the hedge, or something white move in a field half a mile away.

One way and another she and her brother are very much part of our lives. I can't really imagine being without them, but, like leaving my boyhood home, this dear old house, I know that it is something that has got to be faced up to one of these days.

6

Let Loose in a Chocolate Factory
Sixty Brilliant Rides

I'VE already told you how I got started as a Hunting Correspondent, writing up a couple of days for *Country Life* in the back-end of the 1991/92 season, with Woody's indispensable help and a double dose of luck. The time inevitably came, the following winter, when I had to, as it were, let go my old faithful's trusty hand, travel further afield, ride whatever horse my hosts might be kind enough to provide for me, and do so in *terra incognita*.

My first such venture was with the Eggesford, whose country lies between Devon's two great moors. I can't remember just how I felt, driving west that November morning the best part of twenty years ago. Certainly I must have been anxious, sixty at my next birthday, having never ridden a strange horse in such circumstances before let alone with all eyes on me.

As you must be fed up with my telling you, I don't pretend to be a fancy jockey, dressage and all that is pure Greek to me, I just get by with the horses usually doing more or less what I want them to do: but there's no group quite so censorious as riders judging other riders, especially the ladies, you should hear them talk! I must have been scared stiff of cutting a poor figure, getting wrong with someone's pet, perfect hunter, worst possible thing of all, having it refuse at a jump – and what about the jumping anyway?

Then, as indeed now, the long drive to the meet was no doubt almost the scariest part of the whole business. An expectant hunt and a specially commissioned photographer waiting for me: what if the car proved temperamental, broke down in some mysterious way, as cars will, or got me involved in an accident?

If I learnt nothing else at that, my first distant 'away match', I discovered the wonderful comfort of finding myself at a meet, on time, in the saddle, sympathetically mounted, conversing comfortably with some kindly new friend-of-the-day, and accompanied by that all-important person, the photographer. Over the seasons I have teamed up with several 'snappers', as we call them, never a bad one, all to become trusted friends.

As was to prove routine, I need not have worried. "We had poor scenting conditions, did not jump so much as a stick, and I had to change horses twice, but it was one

*With the Vine & Craven Hunt, on Jam, a lovely
strawberry roan lent to me for the day's reporting*

of the most enjoyable day's foxhunting I can remember."
As I was beginning to take in, my new job was pure fun,
in this case especially so because, as hounds moved off
from the meet, the Master invited me to attach myself
to Paul Larby's coat tails. I spent the whole day thus,
excused socialising, silently admiring and learning as I
watched a skilled huntsman at work.

Two of the mounts I was lent that day lost shoes,
and I ended up astride a 14-hand pony called Lucket. This
was the first and last time I ever had to 'abandon ship' at
work, just as, later that season, in Wales, when my mount

lost his footing on Severn shore's shingle, I had the only fall I ever had at work on a loaned horse. I can write that safely now, since I have just reluctantly agreed my retirement from mounted duty with my friends at *Horse & Hound*.

The remainder of that, my second season, saw me once more in Wales, with fell hounds in Snowdonia, later, out with a pack of delightful basset hounds, and, with Diana, stag hunting in France, on hirelings that never broke pace from a terrifying flat-out trot.

My strongest memory of that, and of a second day we had a few years later, both with the Villers-Cotterêts in the Compiègne Forest, is of the admirable *style* French hunting folk put on, in dress and ceremony, and the *music* with which they inform each other of the hunt's usually invisible progress in the forest depths. Hunting in France was like a day in fairyland.

* * *

YOU would not thank me for a blow-by-blow account of my anxious travels and so happy adventures in the next eighteen seasons, but perhaps, again, a few brush-strokes will suffice to suggest the whole picture.

First, however, I must tell you of a piece of luck that fell to me that following summer. Invited to write about the Crawley & Horsham puppy show, I met up with 'The

Captain', Ronnie Wallace, in our sport the giant of his generation. He befriended me and from that day was a tutor whom I could consult at no notice and at will.

In the first of what were to be many kindly lectures over the years, whilst I was literally sitting at his feet on the kennels lawn, when he had finished judging hounds and we were waiting for tea, he urged me never in my hunt reports to pretend to knowledge that I didn't have. He was, I fancy, firing a parting shot at one of my predecessors.

I like to think that it was an unnecessary injunction, since I was well conscious of how little I knew of hound-work and the art of venery, but it was good advice, and I have always tried to remember it, the while struggling to repair my ignorance. It was at about this time that I, a half-educated non-graduate, started reviewing books: books, in almost all cases, written by people far cleverer, far better versed in their subjects, that me.

My response to that unequal situation is to write from the standpoint of what one famous author called the 'common reader', but also, above all, never to agree to review a book unless I have enjoyed reading it, and feel able to praise it.

By the same token, I would never visit a hunt unless I knew that it was enjoying prosperous times, was not in the throes of one of those *great rows* that hunts are sadly (and rather comically) so famous for, and that there was every chance that I would have a happy day. Also, I would steer clear of hunts known to be regularly pestered by 'antis': I can only remember one single occasion in all my outings where they were a problem.

The Captain, whom I never would have dreamt of calling 'Ronnie', was invaluable in pointing me in the right, and deflecting me from the wrong, direction. In the early days I habitually consulted him, when I was making up my 'list' at the start of a season.

Again, and similarly, not aiming to know a complex subject better than those who really understood it, the evening after hunting, often after a long drive home, or on the following morning, I always talked through a day with the man, or in one case the woman, who had hunted hounds, to compare my amateur impressions with what had really happened, to get their story.

Both courtesy and common sense also taught me never to send a word to London until what I had written had been checked and agreed by my hosts. After a day with the Exmoor Foxhounds, in the season following my meeting with the great man, my 'copy', faxed to him that evening read, "Like a seasoned general on a battlefield, he was always moving, without hurry, towards precisely where his hounds might need his help. Through that long morning I never saw him out of a walk…."

"Could we change that to *trot* please?" was his only request.

When I started in this line of work 'faxing' seemed, to me anyway, to be so modern and 'with it', but it was a great relief when electronic mail took over. *Now* what I write, subject only to any editorial improvements, goes straight onto the page, and any errors are my own; but *then* my copy was at the mercy of whatever possibly love-sick, hung-over, Monday morning Miss might have the job of typing it up.

I can never forget the sight of that commanding man, Captain Wallace, who would I am sure have made a good Prime Minister, slowly, intently, descending the steep side of an Exmoor goyle to join his hounds at check: nor the picture of him at a meet, every hound looking up at him as in worship, waiting on his slightest word, aching for praise, dreading censure, longing for the off: nor can I cease to thank him for the very best sort of kindly patronage when I was taking my first tottering steps in a new trade.

* * *

PEOPLE often ask me about what you might call the nuts-and-bolts of hunting journalism, so I will risk telling you a little about practicalities. Very early on I learnt the virtue of visiting hounds in kennel before a day's hunting, meeting the Huntsman of course, and that important person, his wife, getting the feel of the outfit

– no different from visiting a military unit, or for that matter climbing into a strange saddle on an unknown horse; you feel that you know immediately what sort of quality you are dealing with.

More specifically, I have found it helpful, and you may think this a cheap trick, to identify in advance a star hound, one whose fortunes may be followed, if necessary expanded on, if intimidating blank pages should follow a blank day. It helps, obviously, if the hound has some easily recognisable characteristic, like the late Chequebook, my favourite of the Quantock Staghounds. A deer-addict, drafted in from a local pack of foxhounds, Chequebook was smaller than all her kennel-mates. What is more, she seemed to have an engaging disposition. Alive, there was no missing her: I miss her now, on my regular forays onto that lovely hill.

If, in the pages that follow, I seem to give scant attention to the activities and characters of the packs I was following I am merely being honest. I came to my new job knowing virtually nothing of hound-work and all that goes on in kennel, the breeding and so on. In the field I do watch and listen to hounds intently, which is after all what hunting is all about, but, following the Captain's maxim, I'm very careful what I write about them.

A couple of days before my second outing in that first part-season, I spent an afternoon in the Seavington kennels. It was intensely educational, and an experience I shall never forget. There were three smart-looking hunters stabled just behind the Huntsman's house, a few paces across the yard from the kitchen door, and the best part of fifty couple of hounds kennelled at the bottom of the garden.

I felt as if I was visiting a small detachment of a first-class regiment where the young man in charge (currently Huntsman of the Quorn!) knew just what he was about, and valued his independence... his wife, who 'did' the horses, was clearly a vital member of the team, there were children about the place, and a pair of breeches drying on the kitchen range. It was on that visit that I first became star-struck, as I still am, by the ethos of hunt service, especially so in small hunts where there is not much money around.

IN MY second season I had the good luck to be picked up by *Horse & Hound*, and, a couple of seasons later, *The Field* started to give me the odd hunting commission, by which time I might be covering as many as twelve hunts a year. Hoping they will not overtax your patience, a few snatches from my scribbles may give you an idea of the nature and variety of the work.

"How to tell you the story of this memorable hunt?" I asked my readers, after Woody and I had been following the Portman hounds on their last vale day of the

94/95 season. *"I will share a secret with you. A hunting correspondent does not carry all the details of a run in unfamiliar country in his head, at least this one doesn't; he has tea with some of those who actually know what happened, and where we went. It was in my host's kitchen, over eggs and crumpets, with a confusing number of his good-looking daughters milling round, and sundry gurus, such as the Hunt Chairman and my friend the Rector chipping in, that I tried to piece the thing together."*

I ought to tell you about 'my friend the Rector', who featured often in my writing, though was never actually named lest some mugwump of a bishop excommunicate him. We had the immense good fortune to have for our parish priest at that time a man who was not only an MFH, but also a Master of Mink Hounds: like the Captain, but handier – I saw him most Sundays. He was an invaluable sounding-board and a source of expert advice.

Very early on I developed a strong attachment to hunting up north, particularly with the Border Hunt which became something of a home-from-home and which, by juggling editors, I contrived to get up to nearly every season. Here's a taste of another memorable day, with the Buccleuch…

…*"Since I started by writing about dukes, marquises and earls, let me close by recording that the enormous field comprised, with two exceptions, entirely commoners, and that this doctor's son from Dorset felt quite at home.... I need not have lost any sleep over the rather suggestive name, Monkey, of the Appaloosa so kindly lent me. As I rode home I thought of his exotic ancestry, back through the pierce-nose Indians to the conquistadors. To use an expression taught me recently by one of my step-daughters, Monkey was 'the business'."*

I might add that it was not just Monkey's name that disconcerted me. My great aim at work always was to evade notice, to melt as far as possible, and as soon as possible, into the background, above all to avoid being in view of the owner of the horse I might be riding. Little hope of not being spotted, if you will forgive the pun, on a 'Dalmatian' horse that might have graced a circus. Silly me; he was a wonderful ride, and we had such a happy day.

The horse the Braes of Derwent kindly found for me in the following season had an equally disconcerting name. He was an ex-police horse called Inspector Clouseau, described to me by his owner as something of a character. As you may imagine, I found myself wondering what Pink Panther-type idiocy had led to his leaving the public service, and what form his eccentricity might take in the hunting field. Again, I needn't have worried. He "ambushed me at the first fence by taking off about a length-and-a-half from it", but there are worse things than a generous jump; we got on famously.

I had a slightly disconcerting start to the Hunt Supper that evening too. Having asked for a whisky and soda, I was brought, rather publicly, a whisky and cider, which it seemed my duty to down. At least they did not submit me to the torture of 'saying a few words' after the meal, which was just as well in view of the evident Geordie language barrier. People think that, because words come easily to me on paper, I have no problem public speaking; the reverse is true, have you guessed, writing is my *escape* from verbalising?

* * *

WOODY'S future, or lack of it, had become a worry. Full twelve months before my day on Inspector Clouseau, I'd ridden him for the umpteenth 'last time' in our vale. Here's the beginning and end of the article…

"It was a bad decision, taken on impulse, but with arctic weather forecast, and hounds meeting in our paddock, it seemed worth risking one last day in the vale on the old horse."

Diana was off-games with a broken collar-bone, so I rode her super vale horse, improbably called The Bean, in the morning and switched to Woody in the afternoon. *"As we came out of the wood on top of Dungeon and faced the steep dive down over the strip lynchets into the vale, where he had always in the past joyously carted me, he stood rooted and let the mounted field go away from him. I have never been so clearly spoken to by a horse, nor so wisely.*

At tucking-up time that night there was all but a full moon, a clear starry sky, a piercing northerly wind and ice already forming on the spare water buckets by the stable door... I thought not about the weather and probably lost days hunting, but about an old friend and the end of his and probably of my vale hunting"...

....and a few weeks later, out with the Mendip Farmers on kinder going and with less demanding jumps (we took our, well certainly my, first stone wall)...

"My old horse, seven hours under the saddle, all but twelve hours out of his box, left a bit of his feed that night – but then, I found the milk and whiskey by my bed only half drunk next morning."

We were evidently both beginning to feel our years, but then, as I have told you, medicated with 'bute' Woody seemed reborn.

The following season we got on the cover of *Horse & Hound*, every journalist's ambition, following an epic afternoon hunt with the Cattistock...

"...50 minutes fast and furious on the most lovely turf all the way, but with some of the extreme steep slopes that are

characteristic of Dorset downland hunting. One place that we descended, just by Toller Porcorum, was like a black ski run, with moguls. It scared the living daylights out of me – although, or perhaps because, the old horse seemed to take it in his stride."

Dear old Woody, we had a couple more work outings together, but that was to prove his last season.

* * *

YOU must be wondering how much more of this I'm going to burden the page with – so let's cut to the end. At the time of writing I have had well over 120 outings with 67 different hunts, on 64 different horses. Can I just tell you a bit about some of *them*?

When people have been so generous lending me their precious horses it's rather invidious naming just a few. It's a simple fact that I have never, never I repeat, been other than sympathetically, often superbly, mounted; not one of them gave me anything approaching a hard time, not one of them ever refused at a fence, and only one gave me a, completely blameless, fall.

On my second outing with the Eggesford, instead of a 14-hand pony, they gave me an Aintree veteran to ride. I wrote:

"It's a miracle to me that a high spirited thoroughbred could have quit racing just a few short months before and

yet give his rider a perfect day, on a loose rein, in a snaffle bridle, in trappy switchback country."

Re-homing racehorses has become quite a trend, but Mr Christian gave me my first such experience, and there have been several since.

Pikey, a big tri-coloured six-year-old with a pony face and big feet, was bred in Cornwall by a van-horse out of an eventing mare. His very name probably constitutes one of those wonderful new 'hate crimes' and I fancy I can hear the sirens of half-a-dozen police cars converging on me as I write it. Pikey – there, I've done it again – gave me such a wonderful ride with the Axe Vale, that I took the earliest opportunity of returning to ride him again…

In the same way, I went back as soon as I decently could to the Cattistock to have a second ride on Softy. "Here, this is yours," Huntsman Charlie Watts had said as he handed me my mount for the day, "He's my favourite. Don't ask him to jump a hedge, but he'll jump any timber," and so it was to prove. I don't ever remember jumping so much in half-an-hour, or enjoying a run more than I did that morning. For all his twenty years, Softy almost made me feel a boy again.

One of the features of hunting journalism, where what you write on Sunday might appear in print four days later, is that you have no say in either the pictures used, or the headlines and strap-lines that will accompany your words. Almost always they come as a pleasant surprise, a Thursday treat in fact; I have very seldom had any cause to complain with what is a highly professional operation.

"DAVID EDELSTEN ENJOYS A MORNING WITH THE WILTON, AND FALLS IN LOVE WITH A SUPERMODEL", was the headline that met my eyes after riding a lovely mare called Kitty, with the Wilton, shortly before the opening of the 06/07 season.

"Everybody's favourite, she was tall, bay, very obviously clean-bred, and with the presence, outlook and something of the disdain of a long-legged supermodel", I'd written, giving a cue to a no doubt grateful sub-editor.

Later that morning one of Kitty's hind-shoes, fortunately not one of the front ones, was in my pocket; I could not of course have gone further had she been barefoot in front. That shoe, "Cinderella's slipper" as I called it, is on my desk in front of me now as I write, framing a picture of another muse, a handsome twenty-year-old Oxford undergraduate, my father.

That morning was, incidentally, the only time that I have hunted in the company of an eagle owl. Called Steel, it never left the glove, but was a symptom of the concessions made in those early days to the wretched hunting 'ban'.

If I make no other mention here of that piece of utterly shameful parliamentary idiocy it is because my contempt for it, and its authors, is matched only by my admiration for the true-British grit with which hunt establishments have coped with it.

The less said the better.

* * *

HOW did it all end? In the kindest possible way, the Editor of *Horse & Hound* intimated to me that I ought to stop reporting from the saddle. "We've seen enough people go splat this season," she said. Her Hunting Editor followed up with "I'm terrified you are going to have an accident, and I just don't want that on my conscience." We agreed that I would do one 'last round-up' of the four Dorset hunts that my father, my sister and I used to follow in the immediate post-war years.

Here is a shortened version of what I wrote…

"When, on casting off army uniform at the end of WWII, my father chose this part of Dorset for our new home, I have no doubt that hunting, which was never far from his thoughts, was what decided it. Bearing in mind that in those days you hacked everywhere, it was a hunting heaven.

We were in the South Dorset's precious bit of vale, their Tuesday country, no distance from some wonderful

Blackmore Vale meets, with the Cattistock often handy, the Portman by no means impossibly far off, and a free day with adjacent hunts allowed both before and after Christmas. As youngsters my sister and I made the most of it: as an oldster I'm planning one last look at those four packs, hacking in the old style, hoping that you will come with me."

* * *

"THE Blackmore & Sparkford Vale, meeting almost in our village for their Hunt Breakfast, were an obvious first choice. It was autumn hunting and an early call; as I searched for Delphie in our five-acre in the pitch dark, I was reminded of the one special virtue of a grey horse … and of the other side of that coin when I got her into the lighted stable!

No matter. With daylight, super-clean Delphie and I were soon on the road. As we left the village, one, two, three, then endless boxes and trailers passed us in the narrow road. Delphie didn't so much as twitch an ear; do you wonder that I call her Goodie-four-shoes?

You just would not credit the sight that met our eyes when we got to the meet, such a crowd of lorries on Osehill Green, and still piling in, you would think that it was Badminton. There were over 115 mounted that morning, a wonderful turnout of children, and the season not yet even opened.

The sun was clearing the Dorset Heights to our south as Mark Doggrell started the business of the day, his hounds immediately giving tongue, and we were on nearby Loaders Hill when I cut away for home. Forgive me, but a couple of hours with hounds on a keen horse is about as much as I can manage these days.

We had had just one adventure... well, two really. Fording the Caundle Brook in as deep mud as you'll find anywhere, steep down, bottomless plunge, scramble, steep up and out with a grateful sigh thinking "Thank God that's behind us." But then, you guessed it, as so often hunting, back the same way again! Coming and going a couple were unhorsed, but Delphie made nothing of it, bless her.

As we hacked home I thought of the 'BV' as I first knew it. Today's massive fly-fences were banks a clever pony could scramble over. General Fox-Pitt, fresh back from the war, was a Master, a genial figure who always had a kind word for the young."

* * *

"IF I tell you that a very different scene from that at Osehill Green met my eyes as Delphie and I turned out of the stable yard into our paddock ten days later, don't get me wrong. South Dorset Tuesdays must be one of the best-kept secrets in the hunting world. In fact I'd rather you didn't tell anybody about them, because their great glory is that you

can enjoy riding the wonderful bit of vale round Dungeon Hill and out to Mappowder in truly select company.

Prince Charles was in on the secret in his hunting days. We still remember how well he crossed our country, just as one of my neighbours will never forget the Heir-to-the-throne lifting his hat to her as she pegged out her washing. Great days; who could forget those Pulham hedges, or Brickyards, which you must jump clear because of the iron railing concealed in innocent-looking brush?

Foul weather was forecast, and I was praying for just two things as I joined our guests: that our meet would be dry (weather-wise); and that there would be early music. Sure enough, we'd barely quit the meet and were climbing Dungeon Hill when the expected wet sou-wester struck full force. In the same breath a hound spoke: it shows that it pays to go regularly to church.

That evening, in our kitchen, a rather wind-swept Huntsman described the day as "Difficult but fun". One member of the field, returning mid-afternoon to box-up in our yard had called it "Brilliant", another described her day as "Marvellous", and a visitor from the Cattistock said "I can't tell you what a lovely day we had." Dominic Jones was being modest, he and his hounds, not to mention his would you believe it 19-year-old field master, had given a keen field a really enjoyable day.

Delphie and I had been given the welcome task of keeping company with Aintree veteran I Hear Thunder, and Wincanton hero, Ellerslie George, and their jockeys. The three of us had a happy time keeping our reluctant horses out of mischief, watching proceedings from that wonderful grandstand, until I asked permission to 'dismiss' and turned for home. It's twenty years since I first met Thunder's jockey, we were tackling one of those Pulham hedges at the time – I like to think that I gave her a lead, but it was probably the other way round.

Soon Delphie and I were beside the lovely little church that has beckoned me off Dungeon these many seasons (I do go there of a Sunday, but not as often as I ought). It had been a happy morning, and it meant a lot to me to be so kindly allowed to wear the coat that was made for my father pre-war, when I was five years old. It has a lot of life left in it, but I don't expect to wear it again".

* * *

"DELPHIE and I were cheated of our hack to the Portman. Ice-age weather said "No way!" Instead, as Charles Frampton was very sportingly taking out his hounds on foot, I drove the seven miles I had been (sort of) looking forward to riding, and joined as happy and as generously hosted a meet as I ever attended. We were at the promisingly named Fox Allers Farm, below Bulbarrow, the western escarpment of the vast stretch of downland that eventually morphs into Salisbury Plain, it's been part *of my skyline since boyhood. "We're going up the hill," Charles announced, his pack was joyously unboxed, and off we set. Soon the sun came out, hounds were speaking.... and I lost them.*

Most of the morning they were in earshot but out of view. Once I was in the middle of them, once a nearly black hound called Farquhar, who seemed to be a bit of an individualist, flattered me with his company: he was a reminder of the Portman in my Pony Club days, when Sir Peter had the hounds.

All too soon this old man had had enough, but I quit the hill. My biggest adventure had been losing my cap to the fierce, freezing wind, and having it retrieved for me by no less qualified a person than fashionable milliner Cozmo Jenks, whose late father we all remember so well as a passionate fox-hunter.

Charles didn't blow for home until near dark, he told me that evening. "It was great fun," he said, "and hounds went well, despite the poor scent, always tricky in strong wind. I really enjoy going on foot, especially the hounds' freedom, having to work things out for themselves."

For my part, I never had a happier morning hunting, nor in better company. I didn't really want to go home."

* * *

"WE struck lucky on our Cattistock day, Delphie and I, a recent 'ice age' had just ended, but even worse was

forecast. It's a fair hack to Cerne but a once familiar one. We used to get our horses shod there in the days before farriers took to the road.

Quitting the almost frost-free vale Delphie and I found the high downland still 'arctic'. You'd think we'd entered a poultry yard at Christmas-time, white feathers of ice everywhere, drifting down off trees that had never felt the thaw.

It was iron underfoot too, and, as we topped Giant's Head and I began to wonder how dodgy the descent might be, I was ready to quit the saddle, but needn't have worried. Soon we were back on giving ground and entering the village, with seven miles behind us. We stumbled on Will Bryer and his Kennel Huntsman unboxing hounds, and tagged on in their wake, my favourite way of arriving at a meet.

I didn't stay out long, never meant to, but felt quite ashamed sneaking off. Back on the still-frozen high ground, snow lingering under the hedges, I took a slightly circuitous route home, hoping to catch sight or sound of the hunt that I first followed, as a twelve-year-old, all of sixty-five years ago, with the South Dorset.

No luck; and I could have done without a ridgeway raven croaking at us from the branches of a naked ash, because I find my hunting has got to be all or nothing. I shan't ride to hounds again."

7

Do we really know them at all?

"A LITTLE bird told me" is a phrase that echoes from nursery days, it is said to go back to the Bible (*Ecclesiastes 10.20*), but, like so many old sayings that sit comfortably on the tongue and in the memory, it has a strong suggestion of truth. Birds can seem so 'confiding', to borrow a description from one of my favourite bird-books.

I can never forget when the robin that I call Henty, because of the white feather he had one summer in his nearside wing, once settled briefly on my shoulder. Henty always appears when I am working about the place, sometimes hops almost round my feet, but usually keeps his distance, one bright, speculative boot-button eye on whatever I might be doing, in case there might be something in it for him.

On this occasion he no doubt mistook me for a piece of garden furniture, an easy mistake to make, as some of my more sociable friends might say, and his sojourn there lasted no more than a split second, but it is a memory that I will carry to my grave. He didn't mean to do it, birds are not, of course, 'confiding', but they *seem* so, and that surely is a major part of their charm, and quite enough to make us warm to them.

Horses can seem confiding too, but what do we really know of how they feel about us, of what comes back in return for all our love and attention? I often find myself thinking "will this dear old house miss me when I finally quit it, do these trees which I care so much about, and the birds in them, Dungeon Hill, the distant skyline that I carry everywhere in my head, care a fig for me, know even that I exist?... of course not!"

But if our horses are not similarly indifferent, we know very little *I* think, about what *they* think of us; it's mostly guesswork, a one-sided game of poker. But there are clues, and, for many years now, I have been trying to collect them, like bits of a jigsaw, hoping to complete some small part of the whole elusive picture.

* * *

WHAT is it that horses most want? In order of importance, I guess, it is the *companionship* of at least one other horse, or perhaps I should say other equine, because a donkey will do – I even once knew of a horse whose inseparable companion was a goat; *security*, an important part of which I judge to be the security of a settled routine; and, last of all, despite the appearance that some horses give of thinking of nothing but filling their bellies, *food* and *water*.

To what extent do horses value human company? My strongest memory of a lost summer some years ago is standing with Dandy in the field shelter, marooned there by sudden torrential rain. I had him saddled, ready for a morning ride. It was to be our last outing together for many weeks – I was due to go under the knife next day – but then down the wretched rain came, and went on and on, as though it never meant to stop. We were enduring the wettest June and July in memory: it had played havoc with farming, and put paid to my beloved polo club – Dorset's only polo club, started by an old regimental friend – they just could not get on the ground to play.

Dandy is so companionable, so endearingly trusting, when in confidential mood, his velvet muzzle pressed up against my hand, one large, so expressive eye, engaging mine. He stood like a rock, breathing softly, but just every now and then shuffling a few inches nearer, as though he really valued my presence.

There is a statue of a cavalry trooper with his horse in the Royal Scots Dragoon Guards museum at Edinburgh Castle which exactly catches what I am trying to describe, that almost numinous thing between man and mount which would take horses, flight animals, against every instinct, into danger, steady them when wounded even, when surrounded by hellish din and bloody horror in a cavalry charge, so long as they could feel a trusted presence in the saddle, and a familiar hand upon the rein…. failing which, their rider taken suddenly from the saddle, they would go quite mad with fear.

Bella once gave me a rather different vote of confidence. It was St Valentine's Day, when she can have been no more that four or five years old, and I took her out with hounds for the first time. She behaved well at the meet, and delighted me by jumping a post-and-rails with perfect aplomb. We were up on the ridgeway, in sight of home, and it seemed wise to take her there whilst we were both still enjoying the party.

Cantering a familiar meadow below the hill, my mind wandering, she shied violently, and I fell with great force. I remember seeing her, reins flying, careering across the vast expanse of lush grass, disappearing from sight. Next thing I knew, I was in the saddle and on the way home, having completely lost the interval.

There is only one possible way to understand what must have happened. Bella preferred being in hand and under the saddle to freedom, her own exclusive company, and limitless delicious grass: of her own free will she had come back to me, who, apart from her late mother and her brother, was the most familiar living creature in her world.

Company is more important that grub, even for Delphie whom you will meet in the next chapter, the piggiest little horse I ever knew; when I turn her out on her own before bringing out her stable-mates (I hesitate to lead three-in-hand **out** to grass for fear of a riot, though I bring them in all together) she pines at the gate, whinnying as though the world had come to an end, until they re-join her.

Another, more recent, summer memory was of riding Delphie, leading Bella, early on a morning when we had a rendezvous that evening with Mozart at distant Glyndebourne. We were concerned about the rich grass getting to Bella's dodgy leg, I call it her 'nymphomaniac ankle', those of a veterinary bent will know what I mean, something to do with a faulty lymphatic system, I have myself since developed the same problem in one arm. We thought it sensible to keep greedy Delphie in regular work under the saddle: it seemed unwise to leave either of them long idle.

As I led her, Bella's so beautiful head and speaking cyc were just level with my knee, which she would 'mumble' with her lips every now and then. Whatever she was trying to 'say' to me, there was no doubt as to her message for Delphie. Frequent fierce 'ear-frowns' and occasional nips said "Know your place; I should be in front." Yet Bella almost despairs if I take Delphie away from her. Ignoring her brother, she stands moping at the gate yelling for her friend; *così fan tutte* indeed!

Do horses know *us* as individuals? I don't believe that there can be any serious doubt about that, or that they never forget who is who. Edith Somerville, co-author of that wonderful horsy classic *'The Experiences of an Irish RM'*, tells in her autobiography of a family hunter that ended up, as 'Black Beauty' tells us all-too-often happened, between the shafts of a cab.... remember 'poor Ginger'? Walking a pavement in Dublin some years later her ear was caught by a whinny from across the road and it was her old friend calling to her.

* * *

I NEED to be wary of fostering my own foibles and preferences on horses, but I don't believe that it can be denied that, like me, they value routine as an important part of their security, and that, again like me, they are by nature impatient… "Let's get on with it!" seems to be what they are trying to say when any business is in hand involving them. They have that precious thing, so indispensable in a soldier, so often absent in a teenager, a sense of urgency.

For instance, my idea of riding is to pick my horse's feet out, put a saddle on his back, a bit in his mouth and get on board and away as quick as may be. I allow five minutes for it, ten perhaps if there is a rug to be taken off, or a back needs brushing out.

Nothing, in my experience, is more likely to lead to unwanted playfulness and trouble than hanging about at the mounting block. Yet you'd be surprised how many people who say they want to go for a ride, temporise, as though they are waiting for it to rain, or, far worse, for the telephone to ring, who think of a dozen other things to do before putting a foot in the stirrup and getting away.

Again, when I get home, usually I must admit with something in my head that, to quote naughty Samuel Pepys, I am 'with child' to get on paper, it's the same story again. The horses are as keen to get back to their grass as I am to get back to my writing, but all sorts of tiresome formalities, such as grooming, which I regard as downright cruel, tend to intervene.

* * *

I DON'T know what may be your view of popular superstitions: I myself have no time for them; think them infantile. It seems to me that, as long as you are sensible about magpies – I'm sure that I do not need to tell you what you must do if you see a single one, avoid walking under ladders, do the right thing by spilt salt, and always touch wood at appropriate times, I don't see what there can be to worry about. But, bearing in mind what Hamlet said to Horatio, and Shakespeare was evidently saying to us about there being "more things in life" than we dream of, I am not in a hurry to dismiss the claims of those who believe in the paranormal, the sixth-sense.

As a twelve-year-old, at my preparatory school in Buckinghamshire, I was struck down by rheumatic fever and rushed to hospital. At the crisis of the disease I emerged from delirium to find my mother by my bed... I can see her now, remember the colours of her dress. She told me later that she got a 'message', one of her 'feelings', that I needed her: the busy doctor's wife dropped everything, immediately drove to Oxford to be at my bedside. I believed her: but perhaps you will not believe me when I tell you of how I once received a similar SOS from Bella.

It was Christmas Eve, some years back when we always over-wintered the horses in the stable (they live out the year round now) and I had just been to Midnight Mass. Coming back down the orchard path from church I felt an overwhelming need to check the horses. You must know that it was my absolute rule never, ever to visit them after last feed, to perhaps bring them fruitlessly to their feet, raise false hopes of extra grub... I just never did it.

What did I find but Bella on her back, cast against the wall of her loose-box, completely trapped by her own weight, totally helpless and distressed: who knows what damage it might have done to her had she remained like that until morning?

AS I have said before, I hate playing God with the horses, suddenly visiting an unsettling change on them, doing puzzling things that I cannot possibly explain to them, letting them down, as when we start to reduce their winter feed in the spring, or when the wretched clock goes back with the end of Summer Time, and their break-fast is an hour late. I lose sleep over it, knowing that they are waiting there, expecting me, no doubt muttering to each other along the lines of "Where the hell is he?"; I often wonder what they call me at such times, something uncomplimentary I wouldn't wonder.

If you learn nothing else as a soldier you learn to prize comradeship, a good working relationship with those around you based on mutual, well-tried and well-founded reliance and that rare, precious thing, utter dependability. Such comradeship, the bonds it fosters and the trust that it engenders, seems to me to have much in common with the thing that we call love.

So, to attempt to answer my own question as to what comes back from horses in return for all our affection and attention: is it perhaps something even more valuable? Think of those horses with my old regiment on that October day in 1854, asking no questions but charging into what Tennyson immortalized as the 'Valley of Death'. Is it total *trust* that they repay us with?

8

Sunset: the Best Time of Day
Ollie, Nelson & Delphie

OLLIE, a near clean-bred horse lent me for the 08/09 hunting season, was a bit of a rogue. You might even say that 'he had form', as a youngster he had tended to pass rather rapidly from hand to hand, but he was so talented under the saddle, so loveable in the stable, one could not but forgive him. I had him for the best part of a year, came to adore him, and duly parted with him when his naughtiness got the better of me, but with great regret.

Perhaps the best way to meet Ollie would be for you to come for a ride with me? I'm thinking back to a memorable Monday morning one August, when he had been with us just five months, and he suddenly settled, suddenly seemed to admit, "OK, this is home, you're the boss."

Up until then, like the previous year's Derby winner who had to be chaperoned to the starting gate by a stable-mate, when I rode Ollie out on his own he would suddenly 'plant' himself. He would take exception to something ahead and just refuse to lift a hoof, get a little bit wild and alarming, show signs of rearing, should I insist on forward movement. I know such 'nappiness' of old, and have always found that the only thing to do is to get off and lead. But this was very wearying – Ollie was a long way down and an even longer way up – and it was very trying on the patience, a commodity I am said to be rather short of. What was more, he was difficult to dismount at such times, his neck almost perpendicular; and for many years now I have dismounted polo-style, leg over mane, and wouldn't care to try reverting to the approved method, leg over rump, learnt so long ago as a child.

He was always particularly suspicious of 'things' on the road surface. He was, for instance, no fan of the graffito artists from County Hall who leave, no doubt expensive, cabalistic messages for each other painted in stark colours on the tarmac. He would have 'bad drain days' when you might suppose he expected a genie or a rattle-snake to pop out of every grating, and would drop anchor, or he would stand petrified with horror, like matron at a mattress-inspection, at any patch of damp or discolouration in the road.

Diana, as usual, said, "Don't do anything silly!" as I left home that morning, and, although I regard doing 'silly' things as being half the point of life, I had determined on a completely sober, risk-free ride. It was to be a circuit up to the ridgeway and back, nine miles, two hours, road and track, walking and trotting. Off we set.

* * *

AS WE headed south out of the village, up Park Lane, over the shoulder of Dungeon, as always with half an eye open for litter, it dawned on me that I was riding a different horse. Ears pricked confidently, he was walking out bold and fast. "Alfred Brendel, Alfred Brendel!" his mailed feet on the road-metal seemed to say: I being still under the spell of that magician's farewell concert at Plush the month before.

Buckland Newton, our first Dorset home, came soon, with its useful church tower clock, then we continued past the Manor, up Ridge Hill to join the ancient ridgeway, one of the oldest routes in Europe, onto what we call Gypsy Lane, though no map does. In my mind, as always at this spot, the receding figure of Thomas Hardy's Tess is ahead of us. Is there any character in all English fiction more poignant, more real, more *living*, than that poor accursed D'Urberville girl? Do you remember how at "four o'clock on a Sunday morning... (when) the snow had gone, and had been followed by a hard black frost... the ground ringing under her feet like an anvil" Tess took that long walk from 'Flintcomb-Ash' to 'Emminster' (Plush to Beaminster). Ollie and I are at the exact place where … "she reached the edge of the vast escarpment below which stretched the loamy Vale of Blackmoor": how I treasure that sudden sight of the vale that contains my home.

Soon we are over Dogbury with its Iron Age earthworks, and, if you are so lucky as to see them, its ravens, and drop down to what Hardy called the Devil's Kitchen – Dogbury Gate. We have turned for home, leave *Tess* behind us and enter *Woodlanders* country – *Woodlanders*, the book that, in the upper-sixth at Clifton, first firmly harnessed my literary thirst.

We are on "the forsaken coach-road…" where Hardy greets his reader in the opening sentence of that, surely one of the loveliest of his novels. What a clever trick it was to site so much of the action of his stories on a road, his characters travelling, their lives in flux. Ollie knows, as all horses know, when he is on the way home. He strides confidently on, through the distractions of Lyon's Gate and Middlemarsh, asking no questions.

I ride on a loose rein. It is a matter of principle to me, and a rule for life, an axiom of well-exercised authority. It worked very well for me in the Army: I only wish that I met it more elsewhere. Like a good soldier, Ollie returns and rewards the trust I put in him: we part at the gate of his meadow, friends….

.... and so we were to remain. He gave me the most wonderful ride, just when I most needed it, writing up the South Dorset's 2008 opening meet for *Horse & Hound*. Here's the story, much as I told it: watch out for the twist in its tail.

* * *

WE ARE much the same age, Ollie and I, but he has a chest-full of medals... from the Beaufort, the Taunton Vale, a dozen other hunts from Exmoor to Cheshire, and countless team chases. He's a seasoned warrior, and I am very lucky to have the loan of him. It is understood that I am to look after him lovingly, give him an easy life, and, in view of recent lameness, not take him over any big drop fences: he shows every sign of returning the compliment, but this was our first serious outing together.

It's like going back to your old regiment, rejoining the field of your own favourite hunt after an enforced interval. So many old friends greet you: so many welcome new young faces clearly wonder who that old codger in the red coat can be. The meet was in a spectacular setting, behind Dewlish House, and Ollie the perfect gentleman: so far, so good.

After what must have been a difficult slow start for our young huntsman Rory Innes, with a large expectant field behind him, we came a circle back to the southern end of Dewlish Hang, and he called out to me, "Do you want to come along?" Can a duck swim? Off Ollie and I proudly set, maybe his first taste of the plum in the pudding of my job, probably the only new thing I could show him.

We all call it Dewlish Hang, but the map has it as Park Hill, a great long flattened 'S' of woodland running well over a mile north-south, like an eyebrow above the great house. It can never have been more beautiful than it was that late autumn Saturday, the trees still half dressed, despite two frosts, and in wonderful colour. "Settle down! Settle down! Steady!" Rory called to his hounds, then made some of those huntsman's noises that I can't possibly reproduce on paper, and only hounds understand.

The disadvantage of riding with the huntsman is that you must follow him. Rory suddenly took off, out of a track, up the wood's perpendicular side to check on the activities of a couple of his hounds then down again. I was terrified, but Ollie wasn't. We were learning to trust each other.

Out of the wood, coming through the village it was a pleasure to see what looked like the entire population of Dewlish out of their houses to witness the hunt passing, smiles everywhere, babies held up. It was a great feeling, a lovely reassuring sight; I wish those drips in Westminster could have seen it.

Then we were on the meadows below the wood and the fun started. Somebody has taken a lot of trouble fencing that land, stout no-nonsense timber, nice and wide, plenty of room, one a quite tricky double with a stream in it. Ollie was going like a sewing machine, he knew the business. Suddenly I realized that I was living a dream.

Back we went behind Shailes, the first draw, more jumping, the first big drop of the day... and what a drop. I was doubtful about taking Ollie over it, took the easiest-looking bit, even so I thought we'd never land, but Ollie understood all about it. Then across the Cheselbourne road and more of the same, such fun!

It's just as well you don't know what's around the corner when you set off for a day's hunting. Suddenly, early afternoon, there was a cry from behind me, "Your horse is bleeding... badly!" Sure enough, Ollie was pumping blood in great squirts from low down, near-fore. I had to fight with him to get him to leave the hunt, gain the road below us, and work out what the hell to do.

It's at such times you are reminded of the camaraderie of the hunting field. There was a small group on foot ready to help at the gate. One of them was immediately off his quad-bike at Ollie's head whilst I wrestled with my tie for a bandage, losing my father's gold tiepin in the process.

I needn't have troubled. The Hunt's second horses were there. The home team from the kennels took charge of my fractious, dangerous horse, enraged and almost unmanageable at being suddenly taken out of the fun and action. I will admit I was in a bit of a tizz – wouldn't *you be if the horse you had just fallen in love with was suddenly spouting bright red arterial blood as if there were no tomorrow?*

I can never forget the kindness and the competence of those friends-in-need, nor that Rory took time off from his hounds to call a vet, that one of my new friends somehow found a box of bandages, another lent a rug, another gave up her afternoon's sport to ride off and fetch my trailer, and yet another, calmness personified, got on the telephone to Diana, so that a reception committee might be ready for us at home.

What will I remember most from that eventful day? Riding the length of Dewlish Hang, alone with Rory and his hounds: the relief of finding our faithful vet in the yard when I got Ollie home and learning, after an anxious half-hour, that a couple of stitches and two or three days, box rest should see him right: being allowed to wear my father's old coat at the start of its 71st season, and jumping the Dewlish drop on a topping horse in my 76th year.

You may well wonder how I ever came to bear parting with Ollie: the truth is that his suddenly returning naughtiness a month or so later got the better of me. I had had some superb rides on loaned horses that season, then, one Monday morning, with one such ride fresh in my mind, Ollie would barely leave the mounting block, refused to go the length of the drive, half-reared and fooled around quite alarmingly in the confined

*Ollie, the perfect gentleman, when he felt like it,
with me in my 76th year*

iron-railed space. I decided that enough was enough; he needed the company at work that I could not guarantee him; I needed a horse that would go happily alone; if I persisted with him it was going to end in tears or worse.

Last heard of, he was happily settled in a new home, regularly ridden out in company. Ollie is yet another horse that I shall never forget: his, another debt that can never be repaid.

"WHICH would you rather ride, Nelson or Gamble?" asked my friend the Vicomte. It was a gamble indeed, I had never ridden either, and was just recovering from a broken collarbone, following a fall off Dandy a few weeks before. It was towards the end of the 98/99 season, I was on Exmoor for a day with the foxhounds, again for *Horse & Hound*.

"Nelson please!" I replied, for no better reason than that my mother shared that great man's birthplace, the Rectory at Burnham Thorpe. It was a lucky choice, a youngster with an eventing career ahead of him, Nelson, handsome, 16.3, was then strongly dappled – we have since grown old together and are both now plain grey. And Nelson's owner? A Belgian nobleman and Dorset neighbour, the Vicomte Hugh le Hardy de Beaulieu, who has so generously mounted me these many years on my regular hunting expeditions to Exmoor and the Quantocks.

I did have a few doubtful moments on that March morning a dozen years ago, wondered "if Nelson had been at the rum ration", but, the Field Master kindly letting us lead his field, he soon settled down.

By the end of the day it was… "The incomparable Nelson… has Weatherbird and Ben Fairie for his grandfathers (*ie. he was bred for eventing*), but is quarter Highland pony.

He is all class but has the hybrid cleverness that

Nelson, once strongly dappled, but we have since grown old together and he is now plain grey

comes with 'lurcher' breeding": I was no doubt thinking of the beloved Perdita, whom we still had then. Nelson and I have been the best of friends ever since.

* * *

I LAST rode Nelson towards the end of the 09/10 season, following the Quantock Staghounds. As usual, I was 'doing words in my head': one way or another most of my writing is done in the saddle. This time however I wasn't planning scribble, but trying to work out what on earth to say to my hosts at their end-of-season Hunt Luncheon a couple of weeks later. I find such engagements very demanding and stressful, just wasn't cut out for public speaking. Here's part of what came to me to say...

"I was riding Nelson, a horse I have come to love; he has such a splendid optimistic outlook and stride. It was sometime during that rare, sunny afternoon, he was belting along, surfing the blind heather, as I tried to keep up with your Master. At one time, somewhere between Dead Woman's Ditch and Holford Combe, she and I were alone with hounds and it was magic.

Then, later, alone, on top of your lovely hill, there was that wonderful view out over the Bristol Channel. I suddenly realised how very happy I felt. I was just where I wanted to be, out hunting, riding a trusted old friend whom I had known and ridden almost since he was a baby, and in my beloved West Country."

Nelson: bred for eventing, a quarter Highland pony and a hunting horse I came to love

DELPHIE is a little grey cob of Irish extraction who I first heard about in the Wilton country one lucky day at the very end of the 08/09 season. Everyone was talking of this mare, a perfect family horse needing a new home. At the end of the day I hacked home with her owner and got the story: she sounded to be just what we needed to get Diana back in the saddle after a disastrous fall (five fractures). We went back next day; I rode her; we bought her and she has proved to be an absolute trump. I call her Goodie Fourshoes.

As it turned out, it wasn't only Diana whom she was to have the job of nursing back into the saddle. At the start of the 2010/11 season the surgeons had a go at me. "It's like a mastectomy," they had said, "and, for a bit, you won't be able to do much with your left arm." I replied that that would be no problem to an old polo player; they frowned, so I didn't pursue the topic, not wishing to be formally pronounced 'off games'.

It hadn't been easy. I found that an hour with hounds, just pottering around as one does in autumn hunting, was as much as I could manage. Even that got me home totally exhausted and rather fed up. I'd told *Horse & Hound* that I was fit for work, but realized that this wasn't quite true, and wondered if and when they would call my bluff, and how I'd manage when they did. I had agreed with them that I would do one more, last, season, though it was like death to me to think of giving up the work I so love.

My third trial outing, just into September, was on the morning of the 70th anniversary of the start of the Blitz, marked by a 24-hour strike by underground workers. I was pondering the irony of this disruptive echo as Delphie strode up Park Lane, wondering what the scene would be like during rush-hour on that familiar byway's London namesake. An enormously tall cloud stood over the distant ridgeway, Tess's fated walk: it was a gorgeous morning. The huntsman's enemy was just peeping at us, blindingly, over the shoulder of Dungeon Hill as the meet came into view.

Delphie knew very well that hunting was on the agenda; there had already been plenty of telling sights and sounds. We soon got to the meet, in a loved place, a farmyard known since boyhood, were among old friends, and the business of the morning started: "Hounds please!" As before, an hour in the saddle on a keen horse was as much as I could manage, though I felt much stronger. We walked home, dear Delphie and I, the way we had come, stopping only to pick up some pages of the *Daily Mirror*, and a couple of chocolate wrappers, that some kind person had thought fit to decorate Park Lane with, someone who had no doubt graduated from one of our state academies with what I call an 'ME', that is to say a master's degree in Self Esteem.

It was difficult to be grumpy. An enormous, perfect, full rainbow stood arching out across the Blackmore Vale, one end seemingly planted on the village that Diana and I, and our horses, are so lucky as to be able to call home.

* * *

PERHAPS my happiest moments with those horses are in winter, at feed-time, morning and evening, when they are most dependent on me, and most appreciate that I entirely share their reverence for, and reliance on, routine.

I could sometimes do without their forever queuing at the paddock gate, like soldiers at the cookhouse, long, long before any meal is due, and whickering lovingly whenever they see me about the place, as though I had no concerns and duties in the world, other than their feeding and their welfare.

But I love to see them first thing in the morning, before *my* breakfast, when they are patiently awaiting *theirs*. They have been waiting there, I always suppose, since the first upstairs light showed in the house. Now jostling for pole position at the gate of Chantry Mead, they watch me as I wheel the hay nets out across the paddock, and hang them on the tree-guard that is their winter 'coffee-bar'; set out their feed-bowls; then, great moment, stride towards them, cross Locks Lane, head-collar in hand, whilst Cocky, the extremely cheeky local cock-pheasant helps himself to *his* breakfast.

Delphie, despite Dandy's bossy frowns, gives her head to the collar – she is too precious to be allowed to skitter free across the slippery tarmac, she knows that I will lead her whilst the other two make their own way up and across the lane. While I peg the gate back, Dandy and Bella gingerly pick their way towards their breakfast, bare feet on perhaps deep-frozen, needle-sharp ground – we have worked Bella without shoes quite happily for some years now.

Delphie entirely understands the business with the gate, waits patiently in hand, walks gently beside me until it seems safe to slip her collar, then she belts off full-speed, threading the other two with a waggle of her hips, for all the world as if she were carrying a rugby ball, a scrum-half nipping through the lumbering pack.

She and Dandy dive nose-first into their feed-bowls, but Bella always circles hers, then 'sets' to it as though it were her partner in a reel, before beginning to eat. The result of course is that Dandy comes and helps her finish – she never seems to learn, she's so constant, and in a funny way it is part of her charm.

* * *

ONE September morning last year, when we had a house full, I wanted to get Delphie exercised early before our guests were about. I was planning to deliver a treasured hair-slide that a young visitor had mislaid the previous evening, whilst she was trying on Diana's earrings and testing the effect of her various lipsticks in the bathroom, naughty girl!

For once Delphie seemed reluctant to be caught, kept showing me her heels, with sulky frowns. I resisted the temptation of arresting her by the tail, as I often do with Bella: this was just as well, as she suddenly gave a skittish kick, catching me on the elbow of my good arm... imagine it, a metal shoe on the point of the elbow! It was a glancing blow, no real harm was done, though it hurt. Had it been my face the possible damage doesn't bear thinking about. My own silly fault, one lives and learns.

To the best of my memory I have never been kicked by a horse before, bitten, yes, often, and unintentionally trodden on, but never kicked. It wasn't done in malice, or with serious intent to hurt, it was merely a piece of that rough coinage we call horseplay. It had been a wild night, the three of them were short of sleep, her clear message was "Come back later, if you don't mind." You couldn't blame her really; after all, as I often say by way of excuse for their occasional naughtinesses, 'they're only human'.

A team chase with the South Dorset, me on my neighbour's horse, the bold Murphy – enjoying some rural sport in what once prided itself as being a free country!

9

Other Things

IN case I have led you to suppose that I think of and care for nothing but my family, my horses, and this beloved home which I came to as a boy, may I just try to tell you, before we part, of other things that lie close to my heart?

I care profoundly about the country of my birth, its standing in the world, its proud history, its peerless language, our precious monarchy, and the values held dear by my parents' heroic, war-tried, generation.

It grieves me almost beyond bearing to think of their sacrifices, of my father's war-service afloat, at the mercy of u-boats, of my young mother's home-making struggles, at one time escaping death from a direct hit by a stray bomb on her sleeping house, yet to find that the reward for their part in seeing off one would-be tyrant has been to find our country given in slavery to another.

I refer of course to Brussels, and to our homebred bureaucracy, with its massive, shameless 'gravy train' of the self-enriching, self-important, nothing-people who now effectively rule us.

If you live amongst country-dwellers, who rise early, and work long days, tilling the soil and raising stock, so that some of these islands' inhabitants can attempt to feed themselves, what are we to make of those who just farm vast acreages of paper?

How did we get to where we are today? One simple word: *corruption*! As a country now we are as corrupt as we were in that shameful period when the worst monarch ever to disgrace our throne, the ex-Regent, the wretched George IV, son of such worthy parents, battened on his subjects to support his womanising and his gluttony. Does it remind you, as it reminds me, of the legions of so-called public servants who today do completely pointless 'jobs', such as inspecting 'No Smoking' signs in churches, and pay themselves out of the taxes that they levy on our hard-won incomes, of venal politicians who devote days of parliamentary time to fiddling their expenses and 'banning' hunting, whilst the country's economy drifts into ruin?

Who can seriously doubt that the country could and would be far better run by a fraction of the numbers of office-people who today take a free ride on our taxes, churning out petty regulations, inventing 'isms' to bind our every word and thought, in what once prided itself on being a free country?

Enough. You get my gist? It was all said long ago, much better than I could begin to, by Shakespeare's John of Gaunt, remember?

> *"This royal throne of kings, this sceptr'd isle,*
> *This earth of majesty, this seat of Mars,*
> *This other Eden, demi-Paradise,*
> *This fortress built by Nature for herself*
> *Against infection and the hand of war;*
> *This happy breed of men, this little world;*
> *This precious stone set in the silver sea,*
> *Which serves it in the office of a wall,*
> *Or as a moat defensive to a house,*
> *Against the envy of less happier lands,*
> *This blessed plot, this earth, this realm,*
> *This England...*
> *... hath made a shameful conquest of itself."*

How can we ever forgive those who have so betrayed us? But it doesn't do to get miserable: there are plenty of the old sort left, not least in our Armed Forces, or over the nearest farmyard gate. It's high time I went and checked on the horses!

10

A Last Ride Together

WILL you come for a last ride with me? I'm thinking 'back along', as we say in Dorset, to a winter morning, just after St Valentine's Day a couple of years ago. Hounds were meeting at a favourite spot, Harvey's Farm, Plush. I just could not raise the energy to hunt properly, it was raining, and I was getting over a mad weekend writing-up a pack of basset hounds for *Horse & Hound* in far off Northamptonshire.

You'd be surprised how exhausting I find it 'doing' my own horse, and getting it and myself to a meet fit to be seen. Jumping into somebody else's saddle on somebody else's immaculate horse is, by contrast, pure pleasure, and gets you to the meet ready for anything, and home, fit for scribbling.

That morning I thought, "I'll just throw a saddle on Delphie. We'll go as we are and observe things from a distance. If there are any raised eyebrows I'll say "I've just come to check on the legality of proceedings!" I am, after all, by some years, the 'longest serving' mounted follower of our hunt: barely one of them hunting now was actually born or even thought of when I started: that *must* carry some privileges.

Off we set, 'Goodie Fourshoes' and I, by Park Lane over the shoulder of Dungeon Hill, Duntish Cross, Beaulieu Wood, Brockhampton Green, (not Thomas Hardy's birthplace Bockhampton, please note!) Mappowder... how I love those names, and how those old lanes bring back memories! Happy memories of taking my father on his rounds in school holidays, when I was learning to drive a car – doctors were able to *visit* their sick patients, as a matter of routine, in those days. My father worked, or was at his patients' call 24/7, as we would say today, except for Tuesdays, such as this, in the hunting season.

I remember seeing one of the Powys brothers, I think it must have been the author John Cowper Powys, at his cottage door, courteously seeing my father off after a visit to his Mappowder cottage. Then, further on, at what is now the Old Rectory, came memories of the parson and his wife, the scholarly Dr, and characterful, Mrs Jackson.

Out of Mappowder, on the lane to Folly, I met a very old man walking his dog. "You be our old doctor's son?" he asked, though it wasn't a question really, we looked very much alike, my father and I. I tried to tell him how his words made my heart dance, and hurried on before he could see the tear in my eye.

Soon we were at Folly, where the ancient ridgeway track dips down to one of the 'passes' in the Dorset Heights that gave access for downland sheep farmers to Thomas Hardy's 'Vale of Little Dairies', the Blackmore Vale.

I like to imagine the old traffic on those routes. From prehistoric times, people on foot, following the ridgeway, avoiding the mud and hazards of the forested vale; through medieval times, with great trains of pack-horses carrying merchandise to and from London; priests, mendicants, tramping soldiers; droves of poultry and livestock no doubt, though it is not a droveway. A deserted spot now, you don't meet a soul there, it was once a busy crossroads, boasting an inn, 'The Fox', long since out of business but still shown as an inn on my treasured one-inch map.

We follow the old track west, Delphie and I, up Ball Hill, onto Church Hill and Watcombe Plain, with its earthworks, 'camp', dew-pond, long idle 'field system', and tumulus. Now completely empty of man, what a busy and important place it must have been, once upon a time.

I'd heard the horn, just a single note, but, for a wonder, Delphie hadn't. We'd turned for home. Although she had never set foot there before, she knew where home was, the way horses always do. I gave her her head, and we galloped the full length of the plain, luxurious ancient turf, an old sheep-walk that I doubt has seen the plough since before the Romans came. Dear, spunky little mare, who has brought such pleasure to Diana's and my tamer years, she loved the romp.

No doubt she was thinking of cosily grazing, back with her mates: faithless, I was thinking of another horse, of lion-hearted Woody, my 'horse of a lifetime'. For this was the very spot where, all but twenty seasons back, he and I had ended our first day out 'with the pen', for *Country Life*.

By a stroke of luck that I had never had before, or ever have had since, we were the sole survivors of a field of forty at the end of a short but thrilling run, ending up alone with the huntsman and his hounds, just below Watcombe's crest, in Bloody Tent Wood – one dreads to imagine how it got that so-suggestive name.

Hounds were in the vale, running north, back towards Mappowder, when I heard them turn and climb the steep scarp of the Dorset Heights behind me. Whilst the mounted field went crashing off in entirely the wrong direction, Woody and I turned, hopped a post-and-rails, and followed the pack, by then in full cry, getting just the sort of unlikely story an apprentice hunting correspondent could barely have dreamed of.

The story continued… "as the light began to fail our huntsman blew for home, just short of four o'clock.

The best part of seven miles divided Woody from his stable. A gale was getting up, and the occasional dash of rain in my face suggested such haste as was decent with a tired, deserving horse, and a 'musical' loose shoe. Whilst he no doubt thought of his manger, I pondered the fortunes of the day."

Thank you, kind, patient friend, for coming all this long way with me. Good night.

A final, wonderful day with the South Dorset on Delphie

GONE AWAY
The Hunting Correspondent's Horse

I've loved the life I've had with you,
We've travelled far and wide,
We've hunted many countries,
And I've carried you with pride.
Timber, hedges, banks and rhines,
I've tried to play my part,
I'm stiff and slower now,
But there's still courage in my heart.
Don't turn me in some far off field.
With nought to do but pine,
And watch another hunter
Take the place that once was mine.
Bring me in and tack me up,
And fetch the hounds one day,
And send me when the huntsman blows
His thrilling "Gone away!"

Jane Stacy

Also published by Merlin Unwin Books
www.merlinunwin.co.uk   01584 877456

The Belvoir Michael Clayton £20

The Byerley Turk Jeremy James £7.99

My Animals and other Family Phyllida Barstow £16.99

Shepherds and their Dogs John Bezzant 14.99

Mushrooming wth Confidence Alexander Schwab £16.99

A Countryman's Creel Conor Farrington £14.99

A Shropshire Lad A. E. Housman £20

It Happened in Gloucestershire Phyllida Barstow £7.99

Advice from a Gamekeeper John Cowan £20

The Poacher's Handbook Ian Niall £14.95

The Poacher's Cookbook Prue Coats £11.99

Manual of a Traditional Bacon Curer Maynard Davies £25

The Best of BB Denys Watkins-Pitchford £18.95

The Racingman's Bedside Book (various authors) £18.95

How to Watch a Bullfight Tristan Wood £20

We also have a series of limited edition deluxe
leather-bound titles, including *The Belvoir*

– for details see: **www.merlinunwin.co.uk**